engage

Welcome to the first ever issue of **engage**, the new Bible notes that will be bursting into the world every three months, grabbing you by the eyeballs and plunging you straight into God's life-changing word. Each issue will have...

✱ DAILY READINGS from books all over the Bible — ones you know well and ones you don't. Over five years, we'll cover every single book of the Bible! Ambitious, eh? Each day's page throws you into God's word, getting you handling, questioning and exploring God's message to you, and encouraging you to act on it and talk to God more in prayer.

✱ TAKE IT FURTHER If you're left wanting more at the end of an engage study, turn to the **take it further** section for even more!

✱ STUFF Articles on stuff relevant to the lives of young Christians: exploring issues like *self-esteem, money, sex, death, looking after the planet,* and *war.*

✱ TRICKY tackles some of those mind-bendingly tricky questions that confuse us all, as well as questions that our friends bombard us with. *How do we know God exists? Don't all religions lead to God? Has science disproved Christianity? Why does God allow suffering?*

✱ ESSENTIAL Articles on the basics we really need to know about God, the Bible and Christianity. *What's the Trinity all about? What is the gospel? Sin – the facts.* These are the basics of Christianity, and we're going to find out exactly what the Bible says about each of them.

✱ REAL LIVES Amazing true stories, revealing God at work in people's lives.

✱ TOOLKIT will give you the tools to help you wrestle with the Bible and understand it for yourself.

All of us who work on engage are passionate to see the Bible at work in people's lives. Do you want God's word to impact your life? Then open your Bible, and start on the first engage study right now...

1 Set a time you can read the Bible every day

2 Find a place where you can be quiet and think

3 Grab your Bible, pen and a notebook

4 Ask God to help you understand what you read

5 Read the day's verses with engage taking time to think about it

6 Pray about what you have read

BIBLE STUFF

We use the NIV Bible version, so you might find it's the best one to use with engage. If the notes say **"Read Amos 5 v 18–20"**... look up Amos in the contents page at the front of your Bible. It'll tell you which page Amos starts on. Find chapter 5 of Amos, and then verse 18 of chapter 5 (the verse numbers are the tiny ones). Then start reading. Simple.

In this issue...

DAILY READINGS

Psalms: Psongs from the heart

John: Signs of life

Genesis: In the beginning

Amos: God's the boss

Colossians: Life to the max

Jonah: Stormy waters

ARTICLES

TOOLBOX
What is the Bible anyway? 8

STUFF
Looking after the planet 22

TRICKY
Has science disproved Christianity? 38

ESSENTIAL
The Trinity: An inconvenient truth? 54

REAL LIVES
Student Katie Cole talks to engage 98

ENGAGING CONTRIBUTORS

Writers: Martin Cole   Cassie Martin   Roger Fawcett   Chris Jennings
Design dude: Steve Devane
Editor: Martin Cole
Incredibly helpful people: Digby James, Tom Beard, Anne Woodcock, Helen Thorne, Richard Perkins, Tim Thornborough, Carl Laferton

Psalms

Psongs from the heart

In engage, we want to throw ourselves into God's word, discover what He wants to say to us and grow closer to Him, living for Him more and more. And there's no better place to start than Psalms.

HEART ON THE SLEEVE

Psalms is the longest book in the Bible, but it's also the most personal. Each psalm is a very honest song to God. David and the other psalm writers are incredibly honest about how they feel, expressing their feelings to God — anger, despair, rejection, love, sorrow, joy, frustration, thanks, fear, loneliness, persecution, trust, happiness … the lot. Psalms has the whole range of emotions that you and I go through.

TALK TIME

The psalms remind us that we can talk to God in **ANY** situation. They encourage us to be open and honest with God. And they teach us loads about His character. They make us turn to God to remember what He's like and hear what He's got to say. And they point us to Jesus too.

KING SONG

David, King of Israel, wrote loads of the psalms (you can read his story in 1 and 2 Samuel). We get to see into his heart and explore his feelings; celebrate his highs and sob with his lows. But most of all, we get to see his awesome, powerful, protective, loving God.

We want to kick off engage as we mean to go on — exploring God's word; discovering who God is and what He's like; seeing what God's done for us through Jesus; and learning how to live His way.

Please turn to number one on your psong psheet…

3

1 | Two ways to live

There are loads of ways of dividing people into two groups. Male and female. Dog lovers and cat lovers. Those who can wiggle their ears and those who can't. Psalm 1 shows us another way.

👁 Read Psalm 1 v 1–2

ENGAGE YOUR BRAIN

▷ Who are the two groups of people mentioned in Psalm 1?

▷ What does the "blessed" person do? And don't they do?

Blessed means favoured by God, happy. People blessed by God want to live His way, not hang out with the wicked, copying what they do (v1). Instead, God's people fill their minds and hearts with God's law, the Bible.

Meditate means to *fill* your mind, not empty it. Using all your spare moments to get God's word into your mind and heart. That's what we want to do with *engage*. We want to explore God's word fully and let it impact our lives in incredible ways.

👁 Read verses 3–6

▷ What's the result for the person who walks God's way? (v3)

▷ What about the person who doesn't? (v4-6)

People who walk God's way are successful! That doesn't mean they'll be millionaires. Much better than that — they'll become more like Jesus. As we read the Bible, we're being taught directly by God, learning about Jesus and His great promise of rescue. We'll learn how to become more and more like Jesus. What could be better than that?!

Unfortunately, the future's not so bright for those who reject God (v6).

PRAY ABOUT IT

▷ Which group do you belong to?

Talk to God about your answer, and what you want to do about it. And ask Him to help you meditate on His word as you use *engage*.

→ TAKE IT FURTHER

Next decision — will you **Take it further** (on page 110) or not?

4

2 Who's the boss?

Think of the people around you every day. What's their opinion of Jesus? What do they say about Him? Good stuff? Offensive stuff? Nothing at all? Does it even matter how people respond to Jesus?

👁 Read Psalm 2 v 1–6

ENGAGE YOUR BRAIN

▷ *What's the world's attitude towards God? (v1–2)*

▷ *What does God think about this? (v4–6)*

People refuse to let God be in charge of their lives. They want to shut Him out, get rid of Him. The *Anointed One* (v2) is the person God chose to rule His people, as king. When this psalm was written, King David was top dog, but now Jesus is King of God's people. Yet most people reject Jesus as King of their lives. Big mistake.

👁 Read verses 7–12

▷ *How powerful is King Jesus? (v8–9)*

▷ *So what's the wise response to all-powerful King Jesus? (v10–12)*

God won't turn a blind eye to the evil in the world. He has given His Son Jesus immense power, and one day, Jesus will return as the perfect Judge. He will rightly destroy all those who reject Him (v12).

The message is clear: serve the Lord, and *"kiss the Son"* — give Jesus the love and respect He deserves as our all–powerful King.

PRAY ABOUT IT

▷ *What is your attitude towards Jesus?*

▷ *Do you let Him rule your life?*

Tell Him how you feel. If you mean it, ask Him to rule your life as King.

THE BOTTOM LINE
Jesus is King!

→ TAKE IT FURTHER
Want more? Try page 110.

| 3 | ## Prayer changes things |

So far, the Psalms have shown us how important it is to engage with the Bible, live God's way and meet King Jesus. Next up — the power of prayer.

David was king of Israel. His son, Absalom, wanted to murder him and take over. So David was on the run, fearing for his life.

Read Psalm 3

ENGAGE YOUR BRAIN

▷ *What was David's problem? (v1)*
▷ *What did God do for David? (v5)*
▷ *How does David now feel about his enemies? (v6)*

Prayer changes things. David was in a tight spot, his enemies all around him, hungry for his blood. So David cried out to God, pouring out his fears and asking God to protect him. Then he went to bed.

Amazingly, God gave him a good night's sleep (v5). David woke up encouraged that God was in control, would protect him, and would smash his enemies' teeth in! (v7)

God hears our prayers and answers them. Prayer is vitally important. Because of Jesus' death in their place, Christians get to know God personally. They can talk with Him; share their lives and worries with Him; ask for His help; and give Him the praise He deserves.

GET ON WITH IT

Now it's your turn. Don't go to sleep, or go into the day, with worries on your mind. Try this...

1. Tell God about your worries.
2. Remind yourself how powerful and in control God is. Maybe by reading a psalm or two.
3. Ask God to deal with the situation that's on your mind.
4. Get some sleep.
5. Wake up, praise God, and keep asking Him to help you.

PRAY ABOUT IT

What are you waiting for? Bring your worries to God, using steps 1 to 5.

THE BOTTOM LINE

Prayer changes things.
Or rather, God changes things.

4 | Night night

If you want to get in the mood for Psalm 4, put your pyjamas on. David is talking to God just before going to bed. And he gives us us some brilliant advice on living for God in a messed up world.

👁 Read Psalm 4

ENGAGE YOUR BRAIN

🔽 *How confident is David that God will answer his prayers? (v1, 3, 8)*

🔽 *How were other people treating God? (v2)*

David gives us loads of top tips for right living. First, he asks God to hear his prayer (v1); then he grumbles about people worshipping fake gods instead of the one true God (v2); he warns against sinning (v4); then he sings God's praises before settling down to sleep (v6–8).

🔽 *Which verse jumps out and speaks to you personally?*

🔽 *What word of advice on sin does David offer? (v4)*

GET ON WITH IT

What can you do to control yourself when you're angry? Why not make an **anger plan** to help you next time your temper rises. Base it on verse 4.

- Count to 10 and calm yourself
- Keep your mouth shut
- Search your heart and get to the root of the problem
- Ask yourself if you're reacting in a good and right way
- Talk to God and ask for His help

God filled David's heart with joy, much more than any wine could (v7). We often look for happiness everywhere except in God, who brings us real joy. We sometimes think alcohol or good times are what we need, when only God can truly satisfy us.

PRAY ABOUT IT

Read the psalm again.

🔽 *What can you change in your life, so you're living for God more?*

Now ask the Lord's help...

➡ TAKE IT FURTHER

Don't drop off, turn to page 110.

TOOLBOX

What is the Bible anyway?

One of the main ambitions of **engage** is to encourage you to get into God's word. Each issue, Toolbox gives you tips and advice for wrestling with the Bible and understanding it for yourself. But before we learn how to handle the Bible, we need to know exactly what it is. So, in this issue's Toolbox, we're going to look at four major truths about the Bible and how they affect the way we study God's word.

1. THE BIBLE COMES DIRECT FROM GOD

Paul tells us that the Bible is "God-breathed" (2 Timothy 3 v 16–17) — it comes directly from God. Behind the human writers, He is the ultimate author. When we read the Bible, we're reading God's words to us! And Paul tells us we should use God's words to teach us, train us and challenge us, so that we can serve God with our lives.

2. THE BIBLE IS TRUE

One of the amazing things about God is that He doesn't lie (Titus 1 v 2). He doesn't make mistakes either, because He knows everything there is to know. If the Bible is God's word, then it follows that the Bible doesn't lie or make mistakes. We

can trust everything the Bible says. It will never mislead us — so long as we understand it correctly. That's why, each issue in Toolbox, we're going to discover the tools that help us understand the Bible properly. The word of God is the strongest foundation that you can build your life on.

3. WHAT GOD SAYS GOES

Another vital truth to remember as we read the Bible is this: what God says goes. He is the supreme Lord and King of the universe. He is the one in charge. Christians want to live with God in charge of their lives, and in practice that means obeying God's word. As we read the Bible, we should expect to find God saying things we don't like or find difficult (2 Timothy 3 v 16). We should expect to be corrected and trained in living God's right way. You might find it helpful to have a notebook to jot down what God is teaching you.

4. GOD GIVES US HELP

We're not left alone with God's huge book! The **Holy Spirit** helps Christians understand the Bible (1 Corinthians 2 v 9–13). Someone who isn't a Christian won't be able to fully understand the Bible, because they don't have the Spirit helping them (1 Corinthians 2 v 14). We should be wary of the "expert" on TV or the latest controversial book about Christianity. It's easy to bow to what seems to be impressive knowledge, but if they haven't got the Spirit of God working in them, then they haven't a hope of grasping the Bible's message. However, Christians can understand the Bible for themselves, since all Christians have the Spirit. All God's children have access to God's truth.

We need to remember that we depend on God to help us understand His word and His ways (2 Timothy 2 v 7). We can't do it alone, so we must ask God's help. Pray before you open the Bible. Pray when you get stuck and don't understand stuff. Pray when you do understand it — and say thank you!

SO, WHAT IS THE BIBLE?

- ☑ The Bible is God's word direct from God to us. It is relevant today as God speaks into our lives.
- ☑ The Bible is totally true and trustworthy.
- ☑ So we must obey it — what God says goes.
- ☑ We're not on our own — the Holy Spirit helps us understand God's word and apply it to our lives.

Now dive straight into God's incredible book...

Ideas taken from Dig Deeper by Nigel Beynon and Andrew Sach (available from www.thegoodbook.com).

John

Signs of Life

If you want to discover the real Jesus, there's no better place to start than John's Gospel. After all, John is the perfect eyewitness: he was one of Jesus' disciples, spent three years with Him, saw many of His miracles, and heard His life-changing words.

So why did John write this book about Jesus? The answer's in **John 20 v 30–31**:

Jesus did many other miraculous signs in the presence of his disciples, which are not recorded in this book. But these are written that you may believe that Jesus is the Christ (Messiah), the Son of God, and that by believing you may have life in his name.

John wants us to meet the real Jesus, to discover who He is and what His mission was. John carefully selects certain miracles and events to show us the truth about Jesus. They are *signs*, pointing us to who Jesus is.

John wants people to have **life** (v31). Incredible, everlasting, eternal life. Life with God, rescued from His judgment. That's why he wrote this Gospel. So that those who don't have this life may get it. First by learning exactly who Jesus is and then by giving their lives to Him.

So John's Gospel will help anyone who isn't a Christian (or isn't sure) to get crystal clear information on Jesus — who He is, what He did for us, why He did it and how He can give us this amazing, new, eternal life.

And it will help all those who are Christians to rediscover Jesus and understand what it means to have *life* and live for Him.

It's time to jump in and experience life in all its fullness...

5 | The Word of life

John begins his Gospel differently from Matthew, Mark and Luke. They begin with Jesus' birth or baptism. But John takes us back much much further.

👁 Read John 1 v 1–2

ENGAGE YOUR BRAIN

▷ *How far back in time does John take us?*

▷ *What has been the relationship between Jesus ("The Word") and God all that time? (v1–2)*

John begins with a theme which will spread through his whole Gospel — Jesus' relationship with God His Father. Jesus is God and He was with God in the beginning. Jesus shares God's nature; they are the same. But He is distinct from God the Father. *(For more on God the Trinity, p54.)* The important bit to grasp is this: Jesus is God (v1). He's always been around (v2) and always will be.

👁 Read verses 3–5

▷ *What is Jesus' connection with creation?*

Think of an object, any object. Whatever it is, it was made by Jesus.

Or the stuff it's made of was. John wants us to know that the whole of creation happened through Jesus (v3). When we look back at Genesis 1, we see that God spoke and things were created. Jesus is God's living Word, and He created everything.

The word **LIFE** is written through the middle of John's Gospel. Verses 4–5 tell us that not only was Jesus the Creator but He is the life-bringer too. It was Jesus who first brought life to creation, and John is going to show in his Gospel how Jesus brings eternal life as well.

PRAY ABOUT IT

Ask God to help you meet the real, life-giving Jesus as you read John's Gospel.

THE BOTTOM LINE

Jesus is God's living Word — He created everything and gave it life.

➡ TAKE IT FURTHER

Choose life... go to page 110.

6

Goodbye darkness, Hello light

Ever been in the house at night when the electricity has failed? Stumbling around in the darkness, you need something to give you light and drive the darkness away.

Yesterday we read that Jesus is both the Creator of life and the light that drives away the darkness of not knowing God (John 1 v 4–5).

Read John 1 v 6–9

ENGAGE YOUR BRAIN

▷ *Who announces the light?*

▷ *How is he described, twice? (v7–8)*

John the Baptist was not the light. He was a witness pointing people towards the true light, Jesus. We'll see more of what he did and said in the next few chapters.

Read John 1 v 10–13

▷ *What's the shocking response of the world to Jesus? (v10)*

▷ *What are the two different responses mentioned in v11–12?*

It seems ridiculous that the world does not recognise Jesus, its Creator.

And even the Jews, God's specially chosen people, rejected Him.

▷ *What's the great news for people who do receive Jesus? (v12–13)*

You began life when you were born. Your new life, as a child of God, begins when you receive Jesus the Light. And that means trusting in Him to rescue you from the darkness of sin.

PRAY ABOUT IT

Pray for some of your friends who have not received Him. Ask God for opportunities to witness about Jesus the Light.

THE BOTTOM LINE

Jesus brings light into the world. We can receive Him or reject Him.

→ TAKE IT FURTHER

For more about being God's children (v12–13), walk towards the light on page 110.

7 | In tents stuff

Ever been camping? It can be great: fresh air, close to nature, the great outdoors. Or it can be a nightmare: sleeping next to smelly feet, bitten by insects, rain getting in the tent. Bizarrely, John talks about Jesus camping.

👁 Read John 1 v 14

Jesus (*the Word*) became flesh — a human. He made His dwelling among us. The literal meaning of *dwelling* is *setting up His tent*. Jesus gave up His home in heaven, became a human and set up His camp among us here on earth.

Amazing. But why would He do that? Well, that's what John explains to us throughout his Gospel.

👁 Read John 1 v 15–18

ENGAGE YOUR BRAIN
🔲 *What does John tell us no one has seen? (v18)*

There's a problem. No one has ever seen God except Jesus. So getting to know God is a difficult thing. But now, John tells us, Jesus has made God known to us (v18).

As we read about Jesus in John's Gospel, He reveals God to us. Through looking at Jesus and seeing what He did and said, we get to see what God is like.

🔲 *What quality of God is mentioned three times in v14-17?*

God's law (v17) teaches us about God's holy and perfect character. In the Old Testament, people thought they could know God through His law. But Jesus shows us another side of God's character: His grace, kindness and truth. Now we can truly know God through Jesus.

PRAY ABOUT IT
Ask God to reveal more of Himself to you as you read about Jesus in John's Gospel.

THE BOTTOM LINE
We can know God because Jesus lived with us on earth.

→ TAKE IT FURTHER
Carry on camping on page 111.

8 Centre of attention

Some people like to be the centre of attention and some prefer to stay away from the spotlight. Which sort of person are you? John the Baptist knew he wasn't meant to be the centre of attention.

👁 Read John 1 v 19–28

ENGAGE YOUR BRAIN

▷ *Who did the people think John might be?*

▷ *What did John confess to quite happily? (v20)*

The people listening get confused and want to know who John the Baptist is. (By the way, it's not the same John who wrote John's Gospel.) So he uses words from the Old Testament to explain. Isaiah 40 v 3 says: *"A voice of one calling: In the desert prepare the way for the Lord; make straight in the wilderness a highway for our God."*

The prophet Isaiah said that the Servant of the Lord would come and rescue God's people. This *"voice in the desert"* was one of the signs to get ready for the Rescuer's arrival. To *"make straight the way"* is to prepare for the rescuing King. John is challenging people to be ready for Jesus!

▷ *Why do you think John was so humble about himself (v26–27)?*

John was saying: "Don't focus on me, focus on Jesus. He's far more important than I am!" John didn't say much about himself because he was preparing the way for Jesus, the great Rescuer.

GET ON WITH IT

▷ *Do you talk about yourself more than you talk about Jesus?*

▷ *How can you make Jesus the centre of attention in your life?*

PRAY ABOUT IT

Pray that God will prepare you to meet Jesus the Rescuer through the pages of John's Gospel. Ask God to help you make Jesus the centre of attention in your life.

➡ TAKE IT FURTHER

More about Jesus on page 111.

9 | Jesus: the facts

On scrap paper, write down three facts you know about Queen Elizabeth II. Go on, try it... Most of the information we know about her is from what we've seen on TV or the internet.

John, the Gospel writer, is using John the Baptist's words to give us stacks of information about Jesus. John the Baptist recognises Jesus' superiority over him and wants to tell everyone exactly who Jesus is.

👁 Read John 1 v 29–31

ENGAGE YOUR BRAIN
▷ *Write down five things John says about Jesus.*

1 _____

2 _____

3 _____

4 _____

5 _____

By calling Jesus the "Lamb of God", John is hinting that Jesus would be sacrificed to "take away the sin of the world". His death makes it possible for people's sins to be wiped away.

👁 Read verses 32–34

John also mentions that Jesus was given the Holy Spirit. In the Old Testament, the Spirit was given by God to people who had a particular job to do. Jesus had come with the biggest job of all — and it would lead to His death.

▷ *What does John say Jesus will do with the Holy Spirit? (v33)*

▷ *Who does John say Jesus is?*

Jesus *baptising people with the Spirit* means that when He went back to heaven, He'd send His Holy Spirit to live in the lives of all believers.

PRAY ABOUT IT
Thank God for the Holy Spirit, who is now with all believers, helping them to serve God with their lives.

→ TAKE IT FURTHER
Grab some more on page 111.

10 | Messiah message

Today Jesus begins to pick His team of disciples. "Disciples" means *learners*, so we're all disciples of something, whether at school, university or work. But these men would learn from Jesus!

👁 Read John 1 v 35–42

John the Baptist again identifies Jesus as the *"Lamb of God"* and encourages his own disciples to follow Jesus.

Meanwhile, Jesus is doing something that rabbis (Jewish teachers) often did — gathering a group of learners. What's unusual about Jesus is that He picks the disciples — the opposite of the rabbis, whose disciples picked them.

ENGAGE YOUR BRAIN
▶ *What is Andrew's conclusion about Jesus? (v41)*

The unnamed disciple with Andrew was probably John — the author of the book. Through this story he cleverly introduces another title for Jesus — the *Messiah*. After a day in Jesus' company, Andrew knows that Jesus is the Messiah — the King sent by God to rescue the Jews.

▶ *What is the very next thing that Andrew does? (v42)*

Andrew is very quick to share the good news with his brother. Family is the first of several different relationships that John uses to show how Jesus' disciples began to tell others about Him. More on that tomorrow.

PRAY ABOUT IT
Thank God that Jesus is the Messiah, the promised Rescuer. Ask Him to help you be as keen as Andrew to introduce other people to Him.

THE BOTTOM LINE
Jesus is the Messiah. He's the Rescuer. People need to be told about Him!

→ TAKE IT FURTHER
Get the message... on page 111.

11 ┆ Close to home

What sort of news would make you contact your friends as fast as possible? How would you get the message through to them?

👁 **Read John 1 v 43–51**

Jesus meets Philip (from the same area as Andrew) and asks him to follow too. Philip immediately goes and grabs Nathanael, his friend. Philip describes Jesus as *"the one Moses wrote about in the Law and about whom the prophets also wrote"*. That's huge! Jesus is the person that all the Old Testament points towards!

ENGAGE YOUR BRAIN

▷ *What is Nathanael's slightly doubtful reply? (v46)*

▷ *Not to be put off, how does Philip respond?*

Next, Jesus meets Nathanael. Jesus reveals something of His power to Nathanael by showing His supernatural knowledge of him. There's no way Jesus could have known that much simply by looking at him under the fig-tree.

▷ *What is Nathanael's reaction? (v49)*

Yesterday, Andrew went and told his brother about Jesus. Now Philip goes and tells his friend, Nathanael. We don't have to go far to find people to tell about Jesus. Our family, friends and neighbours need to hear the good news about Jesus the King.

SHARE IT

Write down the names of three people who don't know Jesus:

_____ (friend)

_____ (family)

_____ (neighbour)

Think how you can begin to tell them about Jesus this week.

PRAY ABOUT IT

Ask God to give you the courage to speak to them about Jesus.

→ **TAKE IT FURTHER**

Stairway to heaven on page 111.

12 | A week in the life

 Read John chapter 1 again

ENGAGE YOUR BRAIN

Make a list of all the different phrases that to refer to Jesus.

_____

_____

_____

_____

_____

_____

TALK IT THROUGH

Did any of those surprise or puzzle you? Look up what they mean or ask an older Christian you respect.

The writer, John, has used the testimony of quite a few different people — John the Baptist, Andrew and Philip — but all the time the spotlight has been on Jesus. As we read on through John's Gospel, we'll discover more evidence and many signs that point us to Jesus and who He is.

🔽 *What do you think John's purpose was in telling us all these things about Jesus?*

John chapter 1 is similar in some ways to Genesis chapter 1. Look at John 1 v 29, 35, and 43.

🔽 *What is the repeated phrase?*

🔽 *Look at Genesis chapter 1. Spot any similarities?*

John is telling us about a week in the life of Christ. By making us think of Genesis 1, John is also signalling this is the beginning of something new. (Genesis means *beginning* or *origin*.) Since John has also told us that Jesus is the *"Lamb of God who takes away the sin of the world"*, we could say that this is the first step towards the new creation — when all believers will live for ever with Jesus.

PRAY ABOUT IT

🔽 *What one big idea has struck you from John chapter 1?*
Talk to God about it right now.

➡️ **TAKE IT FURTHER**

Want even more??? Page 112.

13 Wine sign

What do you think the average cost of a wedding is? (Answer at bottom of the page.) Were you close? Weddings are big occasions. They were important occasions when Jesus was here on earth, too.

👁 **Read John 2 v 1–11**

ENGAGE YOUR BRAIN

▶ *How does Jesus respond to His mum's hint? (v4)*

By *my time/hour*, Jesus means His death on the cross. He's saying that His most important work will be done later. Nevertheless, Jesus responds to the wine crisis with a miracle.

▶ *What did Mary say to the servants?*

▶ *What was the reaction to this miracle? (v9-11)*

Mary's advice to the servants is good for us to remember too. As we delve into John's book about Jesus' life, we read many of Jesus' words. Are you taking Jesus' words seriously, letting Him speak to you?

This wine miracle was a sign pointing to Jesus' glory — how great He is. It pointed to the fact that Jesus was someone special. Very special. God's Son. His disciples were amazed by what they saw and put their faith in Him.

That's how the gospel works: when people realise who Jesus is and what He's done for them, they put their faith in Him.

PRAY ABOUT IT

What is your reaction to Jesus' miracles? Pray that God will help you to put your trust in Jesus more and more as you read about the miraculous signs. Ask God to help you enthusiastically do what Jesus tells you in His word.

THE BOTTOM LINE

Jesus' miracles are signs pointing to who He is.

➡ **TAKE IT FURTHER**

The signpost is pointing to page 112.

ANSWER

£11,000 ($16,000)

14 | Temple temper

What gets you really angry? How do you behave when you're furious? Jesus is sometimes portrayed as being meek, mild and a bit of a wuss. But that's not the Jesus we see here.

Read John 2 v 12–17

ENGAGE YOUR BRAIN

▷ *What caused Jesus to react in the way He did? (v14, 16)*

▷ *Does Jesus' passionate anger surprise you? Why/why not?*

Jesus is rightly furious at the money-making going on in the temple. It often involved exploiting the poor and vulnerable.

John gives us an editorial note telling us the disciples' thoughts (v17). Look out for these notes in the Bible, because they help us make sense of what's going on. The quote (from Psalm 69 v 9) tells us that this angry incident is about Jesus' passion (zeal) for God's house. God is not honoured by these money-making rip-off merchants.

Read John 2 v 18–22

The Jews wanted Jesus to prove His authority to them.

▷ *What is Jesus' surprising answer and the Jews' response? (v19–20)*

▷ *John gives us another editorial note. What is it? (v21–22)*

The temple was where God was present with His people, but Jesus talks about His own body as if it is the temple. What world-shattering news — Jesus is now the way that God lives with His people!

THE BOTTOM LINE

Jesus is the new temple, the way we meet God.

→ TAKE IT FURTHER

More temple stuff on page 112.

15 | Birth day

Have you ever been in a conversation that has gone completely over your head? Nicodemus seems to be in over his head in this conversation, but he has Jesus there to explain everything.

👁 Read John 2 v 23–25

Jesus did some miraculous things in Jerusalem. But He could see that people didn't really have faith in Him. Jesus isn't fooled by outward appearances. He knows exactly what we're like.

👁 Read John 3 v 1–8

ENGAGE YOUR BRAIN

▷ What do we know about Nicodemus? (v1)

▷ What does Nicodemus know about Jesus? (v2)

Nicodemus makes a good point, having seen Jesus' miraculous signs. But he receives an odd answer — **you must be born again**. Nicodemus doesn't understand. He thinks this means actually going back inside his mother's womb!

▷ What sort of birth is Jesus talking about?

Becoming a Christian means starting a new life. Your physical life starts with a physical birth, so your spiritual life begins with a spiritual birth. Verse 8 means that the Holy Spirit's work is similar to the wind. You can't see the wind, but its effects are unmistakable. Jesus says it's the same with the Spirit.

Being born again changes us. Ephesians 2 v 1–3 shows what we're like before becoming a Christian. 1 John 5 v 1–3 tells us signs of being born again. The work of the Spirit in someone's life is obvious.

PRAY ABOUT IT

Is the work of the Holy Spirit obvious in your life? Ask God to help you live more for Him, letting His Spirit work in your life.

THE BOTTOM LINE

Jesus says: *"Be born again"* — start a new life with God.

→ TAKE IT FURTHER

Birthday surprises on page 113.

STUFF

Looking after the planet

Imagine you're 7 years old - it's your birthday. You've been given a hamster, Howard. He's cute, he's cuddly and you love him. So you feed him, give him water, clean out his cage...

GOD'S CARETAKERS

In Genesis 1 and 2 we see that God created the world and gave it to human beings: to rule over (1 v 28), to care for (2 v 15) and to use for their benefit (2 v 9 and later 9 v 3). So we don't need to feel guilty about eating its plants and even animals. But if we waste its resources, destroy its fruitfulness by over-farming, or pollute it just so we can have a cheap flight to Jamaica, then we've got it wrong.

Sadly, we do all of the above and more. And inevitably the environment, climate and other people are suffering. So what should our response be? Try to reduce our carbon footprint by planting a tree? Use energy-saving lightbulbs? Only eat Fairtrade chocolate? All these things help, but they won't solve the deeper problem.

CURSED EARTH

Back to Howard the hamster. One day he gets ill, so you take him to the vet, but unfortunately there's one big problem with hamsters... they don't live for very long.

Genesis 3 tells us that we face God's judgment for our rebellion against Him. We face death (3 v 19) and the earth is cursed too (3 v 17). So it shouldn't surprise us that we are facing drastic climate change, drought and tsunamis. The earth is under a curse. It is ultimately our fault, not just because we've used too much hairspray or left the TV on overnight, but because we've ditched God's instruction manual for His creation.

Now you would be a bit odd if you started rigging up an oxygen tent for Howard to sleep in, or arranged for him to have a series of Botox injections. In fact, if you announced you were going to have him cryogenically frozen so that he could be resuscitated in the future, then people might start to suggest you lie down in a darkened room.

Hamsters die. This creation is on its way out. But it will be replaced by something even better a new creation. Because Jesus came to deal with our rebellion and its effects, He can make everything new. Check out Revelation 21 v 1 and 22 v 1-5.

This world is not going to last forever. We should enjoy it while caring for it responsibly, but we shouldn't be surprised that it is slowly decaying. As Christians, we know that there is a perfect world waiting for us, one where there will be no more decay or death. Not even for hamsters.

23

Genesis

In the beginning

The Bible doesn't quite start like that. Genesis is not a fairy tale for one thing. Neither is it a science textbook. Nor is it a DIY "how to create the universe" instruction manual. It's a book about God.

Genesis is also a book about beginnings — in fact, that's what the word *"genesis"* means. The beginning of the world, the beginning of life, the beginning of the human race, the beginning of a big problem and the beginning of God's rescue plan.

> Genesis is not a fairy story...neither is it a science textbook

Genesis was probably compiled by Moses just before God's people entered the promised land. Its purpose was to remind the Israelites where they came from and all that God had done for their ancestors.

So you won't find much about dinosaurs. In fact, you won't find anything about dinosaurs – try *Jurassic Park*. You won't find answers to those tricky questions like: *"Did Adam and Eve have belly buttons?"* either.

What you will discover is loads about God — who He is, why He created the world and why He made us. The meaning of life. Shall we start at the beginning?

16 Before the beginning

Genesis. The beginning. The start of something. Birth, origin, source or foundation. But God was there before the beginning! In the beginning God…

👁 **Read Genesis 1 v 1–2**

ENGAGE YOUR BRAIN

▶ *Who was involved in the creation of the heavens and the earth?*

Dumb question? Look carefully at verse 2 and then read Colossians 1 v 15–17. God — Father, Son and Holy Spirit — was fully involved in creating everything.

▶ *So who do the heavens and earth belong to?*

▶ *What are the implications of that for us and everyone else?*

▶ *Why do you think people have such a problem with accepting that God created the world?*

SHARE IT

Why not challenge a friend or relative today: *"Just suppose that God really did create the world and made you. How would it change the way you look at yourself? Would it change the way you live?"*

PRAY ABOUT IT

Take time out to really think about verse 1. We think our world and our lives are so important and significant, but God was there before it all. If you're a Christian, the Bible says that God chose you in Christ *"before the creation of the world to be holy and blameless in his sight"* (Ephesians 1 v 4). Thank God for who He is.

THE BOTTOM LINE

In the beginning: God.

➡ **TAKE IT FURTHER**

For more on the beginning, page 113.

17 | Filling the void

There's something very appealing about a blank sheet of paper, or snow that no one else has trodden on. So much potential. Here we see God starting to make something of the "formless and empty" earth.

Read Genesis 1 v 3–13

ENGAGE YOUR BRAIN

▷ *What is the first thing God says?*

In the Bible, **darkness = evil**. By starting things off like this, we see that God is the complete opposite. Elsewhere in the Bible it says: *"God is light; in him there is no darkness at all"* (1 John 1 v 5).

▷ *How does God bring things into existence?*

▷ *What does that tell us about Him?*

▷ *Fill in the grid below for the first three days.*

DAY	What does God create?
1	
2	
3	

▷ *What is God's verdict on what He has created? (v4, v10, v12)*

It can be hard to believe that the world was created to be good when we watch the news or read the papers or internet. But it was good, and one day it will be again.

PRAY ABOUT IT

Go outside, or look out of your window at some of the amazing things God has created: the stars, plants, animals, EVERYTHING. Spend time praising God that He merely spoke and these things were created. Thank Him that we can talk with such a powerful, awesome God!

THE BOTTOM LINE

God is so powerful that He spoke the world into existence.

→ TAKE IT FURTHER

Check out page 113. It's not empty.

18 | What a wonderful world

**What do you like about the world you live in?
What in nature really blows your mind or makes
you smile?**

👁 **Read Genesis 1 v 14-23**

ENGAGE YOUR BRAIN

▷ *Carry on filling in the grid for days
4 and 5. Can you spot a pattern?*

Day 1: Light & dark

Day 2: Sky & water

Day 3: Dry land & plants etc

Day 4:

Day 5:

▷ *Have you noticed any words
or phrases that are repeated?*

▷ *What do they tell us about God?*

God's creation is a carefully planned
and ordered place. But it's also
teeming with life and amazing
diversity. Check out verses 12 and 21.
Also v24.God is fantastically creative
and fun. He must have a sense of
humour — just look in the mirror!
Think of some of the incredible
animals He created.

SHARE IT

Some people think God is boring.
What can you point out to them in
creation to show them that God is
amazingly creative, with a sense of
humour? Think of creative ways you
can share how exciting God is with
people you know.

PRAY ABOUT IT

Thank God for all the incredible
things He has made. Pick three
that really blow your mind.

→ **TAKE IT FURTHER**

More variety on page 113.

19 | Creating an image

"Aww, look at him, he's so human". No, he's not. He's a cat wearing a vest. However lovely Mr Tibbles or Fluffy might be, there is a big difference between humans and animals. Let's see why in the next few verses of Genesis 1.

👁 Read Genesis 1 v 24–31

ENGAGE YOUR BRAIN
Let's recap where we've got to:

Day 1: Light & dark

Day 2: Sky & water

Day 3: Dry land & plants etc

Day 4: Sun, moon & stars

Day 5: Birds & sea creatures

Day 6:

▶ *What is the big difference between human beings and animals (v26)?*

God made the world and He is the supreme ruler. We are like Him, made in His image, and we are supposed to rule the world under Him.

▶ *What are humankind's two big tasks? (v28)*

PRAY ABOUT IT
Look at how God blesses human beings (v28–30). The world richly provides all we need to live. There's enough food in the world that no one needs to starve, but greed and war leave millions starving. Thank God for giving us what we need to live, and pray for those who are suffering because of war or corruption.

▶ *What is God's final verdict on creation (v31)?*

THE BOTTOM LINE
You are made in God's image. Yes, you!

→ TAKE IT FURTHER
Creative questions on page 113.

20 Under a rest

Saturday mornings, the end of the school year, getting up at noon. Mmmm, lovely rest. Roll on day seven!

👁 **Read Genesis 2 v 1-3**

ENGAGE YOUR BRAIN

▷ How did God view the world after the first six days were over? (Genesis 1 v 31)

▷ Can you spot any difference between day seven and the days that went before?

Has God given up on the world then? Just wound it up like a watch and let it run itself? No, v3 says He rested from His work of creation, not that He stopped caring for what He made. This tells us two things about God:

1. God works

For six days, God worked, and what breathtaking work He did — creating the universe, the world we live in and all its stunning variety.

2. God rests

At the end of six days of work, God was happy with all He'd created, so He rested.

GET ON WITH IT

So if God both works and rests, guess what that means for us...

1. We work

There's no excuse for laziness and looking for an easy life. God commanded us to work and we should throw ourselves into it, serving Him in all our work and studies. Being lazy reflects badly on the God we live for.

2. We rest

Some people are workaholics, they just don't stop. Or they never stop studying. Our work or studies are not the most important thing! Yes, we should work hard for God, but we should also take time to rest and enjoy the great world He's given us.

PRAY ABOUT IT

Anything you want to say to God?

TAKE IT FURTHER

The idea of rest points to something more — God's plan for perfect, eternal rest. For more, try page 113.

21 Extreme close-up

We've seen the big picture — God's people (1 v 26–31) in God's place (1 v 1–25) enjoying God's blessing (2 v 1–3). So let's zoom in for a close–up. An extreme close–up. Zooming all the way up someone's nostrils...

Read Genesis 2 v 4–7

ENGAGE YOUR BRAIN

▷ *What was the man made from?*

▷ *How did the man become a living being?*

We are dependent on God for every breath we take. The tragedy is that we often forget this. Imagine an astronaut bad-mouthing his oxygen tanks or a deep-sea diver telling everyone he was perfectly able to breathe on his own underwater, thank you very much...

We are totally dependent on God and to forget or ignore that is just as stupid, ungrateful and dangerous.

PRAY ABOUT IT

Thank God for giving you life. Ask Him to help you remember that you are totally dependent on Him.

GET ON WITH IT

If human life is a gift from God, think how important that makes your own life! God created you! Try to remember that fact the next time you look in the mirror and don't like what you see. Even when you're feeling down about yourself, God cares for you. Our lives are important. Not to be thrown away in suicide or regret. God breathes life into us!

If God is the one who gives life, what implications does this have for genetic engineering? Should parents be able to choose the sex or appearance of their babies? We don't know all the answers to these questions, but they're worth thinking about. Why not ask your Christian friends what their views are.

THE BOTTOM LINE

Life is a gift from God.

➔ TAKE IT FURTHER

For a breath of fresh air, page 113.

22 | Garden party

Mowing the grass. Pruning the roses. Weeding the flowerbeds. Yawn. But God's garden was not about boring, grubby, hard work.

👁 **Read Genesis 2 v 8–17**

ENGAGE YOUR BRAIN

▷ *What was in God's garden?*

▷ *What does God's garden show us about God?*

God didn't just give Adam and Eve boring, basic food. He gave them loads of *good* plants for food and made His garden beautiful. He wanted them to enjoy being in it with Him forever; that's why the tree of life was there.

▷ *What was God's one rule?*

▷ *Does He give a reason or is He just being unreasonable?*

TALK IT THROUGH

▷ *If God has given humankind the job of taking care of His creation, what should we be doing about looking after the planet?*

Why not discuss this with other Christians at church or youth group?

GET ON WITH IT

▷ *Does this passage change the way you think about work?*

Today, try to see your work as a gift from God and work hard.

PRAY ABOUT IT

Praise God for the superb kingdom He created, which Genesis tells us all about. Thank God that He hasn't given up on us and will create an even better paradise-kingdom when Jesus returns. Ask Him to let you be there!

THE BOTTOM LINE

God wants us to live with Him in perfection.

→ **TAKE IT FURTHER**

Paradise found... on page 114.

23 | Would you Adam and Eve it?

**Man's best friend.
A dog? A hamster? An iguana?
Nope. God has someone better in mind.**

👁 Read Genesis 2 v 18–25

ENGAGE YOUR BRAIN

▶ *What does the man need a helper for? (see Genesis 1 v 28)*

TALK IT THROUGH

It might be a bit cheesy, but v21–23 have been summed up like this:
Woman was taken out of man — not out of his head, to rule over him; nor out of his feet, to be trampled on by him; but out of his side, to be equal to him — under his arm, that he might protect her, and near his heart that he might love her.

▶ *What do you think about that?* Talk it through with friends.

ENGAGE YOUR BRAIN

▶ *What are the three steps which make up marriage? (v24)*

Miss any of them out and it's just not the way God designed it.
One man and one woman, leaving their parents, to be publicly, then physically, united (sex = God's invention for marriage!).

Notice verse 25. No clothes, no guilt, no fear. Life in God's garden was perfect (so far...).

GET ON WITH IT

"Marriage should be honoured by all" (Hebrews 13 v 4).

Do your thoughts and behaviour honour God's design for marriage?

Sex outside of marriage and wrong thoughts of pre-marital sex don't please God.

▶ *How might you tackle your wrong thoughts and desires?*

THE BOTTOM LINE

Marriage should be honoured by all.

→ TAKE IT FURTHER

Elope to page 114.

24 | It's all gone belly up

And it was all going so well. But Genesis 3 marks a major turning point in human history; from now on things will be very different. Before you read v1–13, look back at Genesis 2 v 16–17. Remember what God says.

👁 Read Genesis 3 v 1–7

ENGAGE YOUR BRAIN

▶ How does the snake encourage the woman to challenge what God has said? (v1, v4–5)

When we doubt, distort or deny what God has said, things start going wrong. Think you wouldn't make the same mistake as Eve? Think again.

☑ "Does God really want what's best for me?"

☑ "Sex outside marriage was only wrong back in that particular culture."

☑ "God doesn't mind if I tell a white lie."

God's pattern for creation was Him in control with humans underneath Him, looking after His creation.

▶ Can you see how that is changing in this chapter?

This is more than just eating a piece of fruit; it's a full-scale rebellion against the way God planned His creation. Humans wanting to be in charge. To take God's place. The Bible calls this **sin**.

👁 Read Genesis 3 v 8–13

God isn't asking these questions because He doesn't know the answers; He wants the man and woman to come clean about what they've done. But what do they do in v12–13? The harmony we saw in chapter 2 seems a long time ago.

PRAY ABOUT IT

Say sorry to God for specific times you've rebelled against Him.

TAKE IT FURTHER

Don't rebel; go to page 114.

25 | Free falling

Despite their excuses, the man and woman are guilty as charged. Now in verses 14–19 God delivers His verdict.

👁 **Read Genesis 3 v 14–19**

ENGAGE YOUR BRAIN

▷ *Sum up the results of the rebellion on the following:*

1. Male/ female relationships	2. Ruling over creation	3. Being fruitful and multiplying

1 _____

2 _____

3 _____

What began in v6, with the woman telling her husband what to do, will continue. Verse 16 is not about sexual desire but the desire to be in charge of someone else. And no longer will the man care for his wife as his partner; he'll want to dominate or rule over her. The battle of the sexes started here.

Both of the jobs God gave mankind have suddenly become much harder. Read verse 19 again. Despite the serpent's lies, God always keeps His promises (chapter 2 v 17).

SHARE IT

Our desire to rebel against God has huge consequences. It messes up relationships, as well as the world we live in. Maybe next time you're talking about relationships with friends or family, you can mention how people's failed relationship with God leads to so many problems.

PRAY ABOUT IT

If doing that sounds scary or impossible, ask God to help you.

THE BOTTOM LINE

The world is in a mess because of sin.

→ **TAKE IT FURTHER**

Free fall to page 114.

26 | Die another day

It's not over yet. God's judgment ends with Adam and Eve being sent away from God's presence. It takes the rest of the Bible for mankind to come back.

👁 Read Genesis 3 v 20–24

ENGAGE YOUR BRAIN

▶ What's the good news for Eve? (v20)

▶ What else does God do for them? (v21)

Even in the middle of punishing Adam and Eve for their disobedience, God shows them great love and mercy! And it's totally undeserved. All humans are descended from Eve — what an amazing privilege for her. And, even though God was banishing them from His presence, He made clothes for Adam and Eve, to cover their shame.

▶ What were Adam and Eve no longer allowed to do? (v22)

▶ Why is that seriously bad news?

▶ What was even worse news? (v23)

The man and woman could not eat from the tree of life any more — humans would no longer live forever. They were condemned to death and they were thrown out of God's presence. From now on, they could no longer live with God — they were separated from Him.

Sin separates us from God. We're all doomed to die, far from God. But... the rest of the Bible tells us that God provided a way back to Him and eternal life — Jesus.

PRAY ABOUT IT

Thank God that He is fair in His judgment — rightly punishing sin. Praise Him for showing us incredible mercy and love by offering a way back to Him, through Jesus Christ.

→ TAKE IT FURTHER

More on God's mercy on page 114.

27 | Oh brother

Despite the disaster of chapter 3, things don't seem so bad. Adam and Eve are getting on with their jobs of being fruitful and multiplying (v1–2) and ruling over creation (v2). Nobody's dead yet. But hang on a minute...

👁 Read Genesis 4 v 1–7

ENGAGE YOUR BRAIN
▷ *What is Cain's problem?*

▷ *What is God's warning? (v7)*

Cain seems to have grabbed what was easiest and given it as a gift to God, rather than giving God the best, as Abel did.

Cain was furious and jealous of Abel. So God warned him that sin would take over over his life if he wasn't careful and didn't control his anger.

👁 Read v8–16
▷ *Like father, like son. Can you see any similarities between Cain's behaviour and Adam's?*

▷ *How is God the same here as He was in the last chapter?*

Again we see God's judgment: He won't ignore evil or let it go unpunished (v9–12).

But we also see God's mercy: He protects Cain even though Cain doesn't deserve it (v13–15).

▷ *Look again at v16. What is always the result of our sin?*

PRAY ABOUT IT
Thank God for the fact that He rightly judges evil but also shows mercy. Praise Him for the cross where Jesus took His Father's punishment on Himself so that we could be forgiven.

THE BOTTOM LINE
Our sin separates us from God.

→ TAKE IT FURTHER
For a little bit more, try page 114.

28 The good, the bad and the ugly

You might have heard the old joke... "Cain had to face a fate worse than death — he had to marry his sister!" We're not given any details about where Cain manages to find a wife, but within a few generations, the population is growing nicely. Or should that be nastily?

👁 **Read Genesis 4 v 17–24**

ENGAGE YOUR BRAIN

▷ *What positive things are Cain's descendants involved in? (v20–22)*

▷ *What negative things do they get up to?*

▷ *Why is Lamech's attitude so bad? (v23–24)*

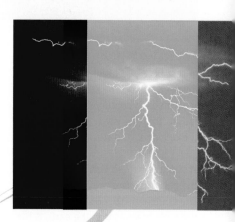

Despite some of the progress that seems to be going on, mankind is still messed up by sin: bigamy, murder and pride, just to pick three.

▷ *How is today's world similar?*

👁 **Read v 25–26**

▷ *What signs of hope can you spot?*

God has mercy on Adam and Eve as individuals, giving them another child. But people in general also start calling *"on the name of the Lord."*

PRAY ABOUT IT

Thank God that however bad the world gets, there are still people who do turn to Him. Pray for people you know who are living without God, that they would learn to call on His name, and start living for Him.

THE BOTTOM LINE

The world without God is in a downward spiral.

→ **TAKE IT FURTHER**

Find the Genesis pattern on p114.

Has science disproved Christianity?

Each issue in TRICKY, we tackle some of those mind-bendingly tricky questions that confuse us all, as well as questions that friends bombard us with. First up... Hasn't science disproved Christianity?

SCIENCE V CHRISTIANITY

In school, we're taught that the earth revolves around the sun. But before the sixteenth century, everyone was taught that the earth is the centre of the universe, and the sun orbits it.

A scientist named Galileo argued that the earth revolves around the sun. The church in Galileo's day claimed the Bible teaches that the earth is the centre of the universe — even though the Bible says no such thing! We now know that Galileo was completely right. Critics of the church haven't let Christians forget this. Since then, many scientists have questioned the credibility of Christianity.

In 1859, Charles Darwin proposed his theory of evolution by natural selection. He suggested that species which adapted best to their environment were most likely to live long enough to reproduce and pass on those "survival characteristics"

to the next generation. Darwin suggested that if this process occurred over millions of years, it might account for the many different species found on the earth.

This theory was great news for atheists. For them, life on earth could be explained without the existence of a Creator God. All living things, including humans, could have simply evolved from the same "primordial soup". (Interestingly, Darwin himself didn't deny the existence of God!)

SCIENCE V CHRISTIANITY

Many people seem to think it's ridiculous to believe in God. *"Surely science has proved there is no God."* And yet many influential scientists are Christians. And many who aren't acknowledge the possibility of God's existence. Isaac Newton, Michael Faraday and Louis Pasteur all had faith in God. Leading astrobiologist Paul Davies wouldn't claim to be a

Christian, yet he's convinced that the nature of the universe can only be explained by the existence of a supremely intelligent being — God.

Many scientists have stated that what Christians have being saying for centuries does in fact fit the big scientific picture for the universe. This doesn't prove God's existence, but it does suggest that science and Christianity don't have to be enemies. Believing in God is not unscientific.

THE HOW AND WHY

Science and Christianity look at and explain things from different angles. Science looks at **how** things happen, devising theories to explain how things work. But Christianity looks at **why** things happen.

For example, I could ask the question: *"Why is this window broken?"* Science explains **how**: when a missile weighing 500 grams, travelling at 50mph, strikes a pane of glass 2mm thick, the glass will shatter. The **why** answer is that Josh miskicked the football and it smashed the window. Both of these explanations are correct, but we're looking at the event from different angles. Similarly, science is great at speculating about the big **how** of the universe, but we must turn elsewhere for the **why.**

Science can't state whether God is behind the universe or not, because

this isn't a scientific question. As thinking human beings, scientists will have views on this topic, but science does not and cannot disprove Christianity. Nor does it prove it to be true. Science and Christianity look at the universe from different viewpoints, and ask different sets of important questions.

BACK TO THE BIBLE

God knows all about science. He hasn't said anything in the Bible that contradicts established scientific fact. God created everything, so we should marvel at His wonderful universe and investigate how it all works.

So, science has not disproved Christianity and the two don't have to be enemies. Christians believe that the answers to the big questions in life are found in the Bible, and ultimately in Jesus. And we don't need to be embarrassed about it!

Amos

God's the boss

Let's set the scene. It's about 750 years before Jesus will be born. God's nation of Israel has split into two kingdoms — Judah in the south and Israel in the north.

Enter Amos. He was around at a similar time to Jonah (who we'll read about later). Amos was a shepherd in Judah, but God sent him to Israel to deliver the Lord's hard-hitting words. Israel was doing well — the nation was wealthy, strong and safe. But the rich were corrupt, mistreating the poor and disobeying God. OK, so they were keeping religious traditions, but their lives were full of sin, living for themselves and not for God.

Through His prophet, Amos, God told His people this couldn't continue. God was angry with them. He had done so much for them, but they threw it all back in His face. Amos brought this message to Israel — *"You've messed up, you've angered God and you're going to be punished."*

Amos' message is just as strong to God's people today; our God is no push-over. He's a God who cares about right and wrong and won't let wrong-doers get away with it. So it's high time His people listened very carefully to what He's got to say. And started living in the light of His judgment.

Bring it on, Amos.

29 | Roar material

What makes you angry?
What really drives you mad?
Over the next two weeks, we'll discover
what brings out God's holy anger.

Our anger can be sin-filled, and self-serving. We're often angry because we feel badly treated and it helps relieve our frustrations to strike out at people. In Amos, God confronts people who are caught up in their own worries, but not concerned about bigger issues like social justice and helping the poor.

God's anger comes out of His love for His people and His desire for them to serve Him. And His desire for everyone to be treated fairly, especially the poor and mistreated.

But before all that, let's meet Amos…

👁 Read Amos 1 v 1–2

ENGAGE YOUR BRAIN
▶ *What do we learn about Amos?*

Amos' biography is just one verse long! We know he lived in Judah, but took God's message to Israel, just before a big earthquake. Unlike most of God's messengers, he wasn't a full-time prophet, but a shepherd chosen by God to speak to the people of Israel. And that's it. We don't need to know any more, because Amos' **message** is the important thing.

▶ *How is God described in verse 2?*
▶ *How does this image fit with your picture of God?*

The Lord roars like a lion — He is angry with His people. He rescued them, led them and showed them His glory in His holy city (Jerusalem/Zion). But His people did their own thing and worshipped other gods. So now God's angry, and after His roar will come judgment.

PRAY ABOUT IT
How do you view God? As a distant, invisible being? As a loving old man? Or as a roaring lion? Ask God to reveal what He's really like to you as you read His message in Amos.

→ TAKE IT FURTHER
Find the lion on page 115.

41

30 Nasty neighbours

Israel was God's nation. God had a covenant agreement with them: He would lead them, protect them and defeat their enemies. Israel's part of the covenant was to obey God, living with Him as their King.

Well, God kept His side of the deal…

Read Amos 1 v 3 – 2 v 3

ENGAGE YOUR BRAIN

▶ *What were the sins of Israel's enemies?*

Check out the map on page 40. No wonder God didn't hold back His wrath (punishment) from these disgusting nations.

Syria (Damascus) slaughtered the people of Gilead; Philistia (Gaza) and Phoenicia (Tyre) sold whole communities into slavery; Edom attacked God's people; Ammon slaughtered whole nations (including pregnant women) to become more powerful; and Moab was just as cruel as the others.

Because of their sins, God would destroy these nations.

▶ *How do you think the Israelites felt, hearing their evil enemies would be destroyed?*

God hates sin and He rightly punishes it. The Israelites were probably feeling smug about all this, but tomorrow we'll read how God's anger turned on them too. It's easy to think other people are much more sinful than we are, but we have to concentrate on serving God in our own lives.

PRAY ABOUT IT

Praise God that He is fair in His judgment. Ask Him to intervene in situations around the world where nations are acting cruelly.

THE BOTTOM LINE

God hates sin and will punish it.

→ TAKE IT FURTHER

Go worldwide on page115.

31 Spot the difference

Yesterday we read of God's furious anger against Israel's enemies for their terrible sins. But it turns out that God's people (Judah and Israel) were no better!

👁 **Read Amos 2 v 4–8**

ENGAGE YOUR BRAIN

▶ *What had Judah and Israel done wrong?*

▶ *They were God's people, but were they any better than the other nations?*

▶ *Why should they have been different?*

👁 **Read verses 9–16**

▶ *What had God done for Israel? (v9–11)*

▶ *How had Israel repaid God? (v12, v6–8)*

▶ *So what would God do? (v13–16)*

For centuries, the Lord had led His people, showing them great love and protection. He defeated their powerful enemies, rescued them from Egypt (Exodus 12–14), and gave them prophets and holy men to help them live His way (v11). But the Israelites had not listened to these people and they'd disobeyed God in every way possible (v6–8). So God would punish His people just like every other ungrateful, disobedient nation.

Every nation will be judged by God, one day. Yes, even this one. People must live in the light of this judgment, knowing that God punishes those who go against Him. As Christians, we're expected to be different. God has done so much for us, and we should want to show our thanks by obeying Him, living His way.

PRAY ABOUT IT

Spend time thanking God for many of the things He's done for you. Tell Him how you feel about the way you're living right now. Be honest.

THE BOTTOM LINE

God's people should be different.

→ **TAKE IT FURTHER**

Want more? Head to page 115.

32 | Special treatment

Your parents are away for the evening, so you have a bit of a party. A few things get broken and the place gets trashed. Suddenly, your mother walks in... All of you are guilty, but who will her fury be directed at most — you or your friends?

👁 Read Amos 3 v 1–10

ENGAGE YOUR BRAIN

▷ *What was special about the Israelites? (v2)*

▷ *Did they live like God's chosen people? (v9–10)*

God chose the Israelites, out of all the people in the world, to be His own people, to be like Him, to be holy. But we know how they behaved (see yesterday's *engage*). God had warned His people so many times (v6–8), but they still ignored Him. He'd been so patient with them, but time was running out for Israel.

👁 Read v11–15

▷ *How will God punish Israel? (v11)*

▷ *What protection will their religion and wealth give them? (v14–15)*

Israel had repeatedly turned away from God. So God would let an enemy (Assyria) destroy them (v11). Only a few would survive (v12). They couldn't hide behind their fake religion (v14) and their wealth and big houses would count for nothing (v15).

THE BOTTOM LINE
God judges His own people more strictly than others. The privilege of being chosen by Him carries the responsibility of living for Him.

GET ON WITH IT
▷ *Bearing this in mind, what changes do you need to make in your life?*

PRAY ABOUT IT
Go on then, tell God...

➡ TAKE IT FURTHER
On page 115.

33 | Silly cows

"You beautiful cow". Would you take that as a compliment or an insult? Amos compared the rich women of Samaria to the best breed of cattle! They may even have been flattered, but Amos didn't have anything good to say about them.

👁 Read Amos 4 v 1–3

ENGAGE YOUR BRAIN

▷ What did these women/cows do wrong?

▷ What would happen to them?

Amos compared these wealthy women to the best cows: sleek, well-fed, spoiled. They mistreated the poor and needy, caring more about what they were drinking. Well, it's very easy to fall for the good things in life. But God would punish them — they would be led away from His presence.

GET ON WITH IT

▷ How do you treat the poor and needy?

▷ What positive things can you do for someone worse off than you?

👁 Read verses 4–5

They were really religious. They gave all the right sacrifices and felt so good about it. But it was false religion. Back home, they were not living for God. They were oppressing the poor and grabbing good things for themselves.

TALK IT THROUGH

Grab some Christian friends and discuss this:

• What do we do out of duty and what do we do out of love for God?

• How should our church life affect our home life more?

• What positive action will we take?

PRAY ABOUT IT

You must have loads to talk to God about today, right?

→ TAKE IT FURTHER

Mooove to page 115. Sorry.

Warning signs

BEWARE OF THE DOG!
CAUTION: SLIPPERY FLOOR
CAREFUL – EXPLODING FROGS OVERHEAD!
Do you listen to warnings? The Israelites didn't.

👁 Read Amos 4 v 6–11

ENGAGE YOUR BRAIN

▷ *What five warnings/punishments did God hit Israel with?*

▷ *What was their response? (v6, 8, 9, 10, 11)*

The Israelites were God's chosen people. They should have been worshipping God with their whole lives. But they lived their own way instead, like naughty, stubborn children. God punished them again and again, yet they still refused to return to Him. Crazy! God gave them so many chances.

By the way, this doesn't mean that all the bad things that happen to Christians are God punishing us! This was God sending a specific message to His people in Israel.

👁 Read verses 12–13

▷ *What must Israel prepare for? (v12)*

▷ *How would you describe God from the picture in v13?*

The people were religious and kept all the traditions and rituals. But they were not worshipping God in the way they lived. One day they would meet God face to face (v12). And they'd have to answer for the way they rejected Him.

We'll all meet God one day. And what a God! He creates mountains. He rules the universe. He's not to be messed with! The question is this: **Have we given our lives to Him or have we lived our own way?** One day, powerful, almighty God will want to know the answer.

THE BOTTOM LINE

One day, everyone will face our awesome, terrifying, perfect, almighty God.

→ TAKE IT FURTHER

Read the signs. They say:
GO DIRECTLY TO PAGE 115.

35 | Dead serious

**Israel refused to turn back to God,
so God would judge them. Time for the funeral...**

👁 **Read Amos 5 v 1–3**

It's as if Israel is already dead.
They've turned against God, so God
will destroy them. Is there anything
Israel can do? Is there any hope?

👁 **Read verses 4–17**

ENGAGE YOUR BRAIN

▷ *Here we read more of the terrible
things Israel did. What were they?
(v10–13)*

▷ *So what should they do (v4–6)?*

▷ *What hope was there for Israel?
(v14–15)*

God's people had turned away from
Him. They'd ignored all His warnings
and chosen to live their own way.
They'd hidden behind religion,
thinking God was with them, but He
wasn't. They were religious, going
to the temples in Bethel, Gilgal and
Beersheba (v5). But they didn't obey
God at all. They deserved to be
destroyed.

And yet God gives them another
lifeline: *"Seek me and live... seek
good, not evil... perhaps the Lord
God Almighty will have mercy"*.
Despite all the terrible things
they'd done, God still wanted them
to turn back to Him. To live His way.
He wanted to rescue them, not
destroy them.

THE BOTTOM LINE

It's never too late to turn back to
the Lord! He sent Jesus so that we
can believe in Him and have our sins
forgiven. It's not too late!

PRAY ABOUT IT

It's time to do business with God.
Tell Him how you feel you're living
right now. Tell Him what you're
going to do about it. Ask His help,
and don't stop asking.

⇨ **TAKE IT FURTHER**

Want some more?
Check out page 115.

36 | Losing your religion

Leann's having a bad day in the great outdoors. She managed to escape a mountain lion only to run into a bear. And when she got safely home and rested against the wall ... a rattlesnake bit her.

A weird story I know, but that's how God describes Israel.

👁 Read Amos 5 v 18–20

They thought God would reward them because they were His people. But when the day of the Lord comes, Jesus will judge them and punish them for going against God.

👁 Read verses 21–27

ENGAGE YOUR BRAIN

▶ What did God think of their fake religion? (v21–22)

▶ What would happen to them? (v27)

▶ What does God want from His people, rather than religious rituals? (v24)

Turning up at church on Sunday, singing songs and appearing holy is not what God wants from us. In verse 24, Amos tells us what God wants — **justice** (treating everyone fairly) and **righteousness** (obeying God, living His way). It's good to go to church, to sing to God and all of that. But God requires us to live our **WHOLE LIVES** for Him, not just our Sundays.

The great news for Christians is that Jesus has given us His righteousness — He's made us right with God. So we don't need to fear the day of the Lord; we're already forgiven!

GET ON WITH IT

☑ Think about what you're like on Sundays and in Christian meetings.

☑ Now think about what you're like the rest of the time.

☑ Is there a difference?

☑ What will you do about that?

→ TAKE IT FURTHER

Pop over to page 116 for some pertinent prayer pointers.

37 | Easy life?

What's the biggest punishment you've had? I once had to write I WILL NOT MAKE A NOISE LIKE A HISSING SNAKE 100 times, for impersonating a gas tap in a science lesson. But God is giving His people some SERIOUS discipline...

👁 Read Amos 6 v 1–7

ENGAGE YOUR BRAIN

▷ *What was God's criticism of Israel's leaders? (v4–6)*

▷ *What will their punishment be (v7)*

These guys had an easy life. They weren't getting into serving God or helping out the poor and needy. They spent all their time stuffing their faces, playing music, getting drunk and beautifying themselves.

Ever fall into that trap? Enjoying life too much and leaving God out of the picture? But God would take it all away from the Israelites and kick them out of their country (v7).

GET ON WITH IT

▷ *What selfish things in your life will you drop?*

▷ *Think of things to do instead that please God.*

👁 Read verses 8–14

▷ *What else was Israel (also called "Jacob") guilty of? (v8)*

They didn't even praise God when He gave them victory — they took all the glory themselves (v13). They were so full of themselves, God didn't even get a mention (v10). The questions in verse 12 are strange, but Amos is saying: *"How can you put wealth and military victory over social justice and right living???"*

THE BOTTOM LINE

Christians can't accept Jesus' rescue from sin and then live as if it didn't matter.

PRAY ABOUT IT

Pray about what you've discovered today.

→ TAKE IT FURTHER

Find fame and power on page 116.

38 | Priest v Prophet

**Has anyone ever teased you for your beliefs?
Amos is about to be attacked by a priest!
But first, he has three vivid visions...**

👁 Read Amos 7 v 1–9

ENGAGE YOUR BRAIN

▷ What punishment was being threatened? (v1, 4, 9)

▷ Why did God stop ("relent") the first two times? (v2, 5)

Israel (also called "Jacob") deserved to be punished. But twice Amos prayed to God, asking Him not to destroy the land. God answered the prayers. But the third time, God didn't back down. He had built Israel perfectly, like a straight wall. Now He would see who wasn't living His way and they'd be punished. God's judgment is accurate and fair.

👁 Read verses 10–17

Amaziah was supposed to be a priest serving God, but he rejected God's message! Unbelievable. Yet Amos (a mere shepherd) obeyed God and left his home to take God's message to a nation that didn't want to listen.

AMAZIAH	AMOS
Hated God's message (v10)	Delivered God's message, even though it was unpleasant (v15)
Lied about God's servant (v10)	Was sent by God (v15)
Attacked God's messenger (v12)	Spoke against God's enemy (v16–17)
Pretended to be serving God (v13)	

PRAY ABOUT IT

There are two ways to live. Rejecting God like Amaziah, or living His way like Amos. Talk to God about the way you've chosen.

→ TAKE IT FURTHER

Grab some more on page 116.

39 | Silent plight

Amos has been talking loads about judgment. God's judgment against His disobedient people. You may think "Big deal, so what?" Now Amos hits us between the eyes with how serious and awful God's justice is.

👁 Read Amos 8 v 1–10

ENGAGE YOUR BRAIN

▶ How would you describe God's punishment of those who reject Him? (v2–3, 8–10)

They refused to live God's way, didn't care for the poor and grabbed as much as they could. For this they'd be punished. They wanted to live their lives without God, so God would give them what they wanted. They'd be without Him for ever. And it would be HORRIBLE.

👁 Read verses 11–14

▶ What would God take away from His people? (v11–12)

That's the worst kind of famine. Imagine life without the Bible, without knowing about Jesus, without God's teaching, encouragement and love. Silence. Total, painful, unbearable, godless silence.

GET ON WITH IT

▶ How much do you value God's word?

▶ What steps can you take to hear it and understand it more?

▶ Who do you know who refuses to live God's way?

▶ What do they face if they keep rejecting God?

▶ What will you pray for them?

THE BOTTOM LINE

God's judgment will be horrible, but deserved by those who reject Him.

→ TAKE IT FURTHER

Shhhh. Tiptoe to page 116 for more…

40 No escape

**There has been a lot of doom and gloom in Amos.
If you want a happy ending, skip to tomorrow's study.
Because Amos isn't holding back in today's message...**

👁 Read Amos 9 v 1-6

ENGAGE YOUR BRAIN

▷ *Will there be any escape from God's judgment? (v1–4)*

▷ *Why not?*

The Israelites had worshipped fake gods instead of the God who had done everything for them. So He would bring their temples down on their heads (v1). There would be no escape for God's enemies.

Read slowly through verses 5–6.
▷ *This is our God. How do we treat Him lightly or ignore Him?*

👁 Read verses 7–10

God had rescued Israel from their enemies (v7). They owed Him everything and yet they gave Him nothing. They treated Him just as every godless nation did.

So God would sift through them and reject all those who rejected Him (v9–10). But there was still hope — some would be rescued (v8).

God's final judgment day is coming. Those who fail to take sin seriously and don't see that it needs a cure will not escape God's punishment. (Check out Hebrews 10 v 26–31.) For the good news of the cure, see tomorrow's *engage*…

PRAY ABOUT IT
What do you need to pray…
a) for yourself?
b) for people around you who ignore God?
c) for people at church who don't really live for God all the time?

THE BOTTOM LINE
There is no escape from God's judgment. Unless… (see tomorrow!)

→ TAKE IT FURTHER
Escape to page 116.

41 Future fantastic

How would you describe Amos' message so far? Angry? Depressing? Barking mad? Heavy-going? Amos's message to Israel has been uncomfortable reading — God's people would be punished for rejecting God.

Surprisingly, Amos signs off with a positive picture of the future.

👁 **Read Amos 9 v 11–12**

ENGAGE YOUR BRAIN
▶ *Any idea what that's all about? Wanna guess?*

Israel had once been a great, godly nation under God's chosen king, David (v11). Amos is hinting that one day, God's King (Jesus, who was descended from David) will come and rule forever. God's enemies (Edom in v12) will be defeated and Jesus will rule all of God's people in the perfect kingdom.

👁 **Read verses 13–15**
▶ *What will life be like for God's people after God's judgment? (v13–15)*

The world has been wrecked by sin. The evidence is all around us: famine, greed, wars, violence, depression. But when Jesus comes back, sin will be dealt with once and for all. And God's people (Christians) will live forever in the perfect, restored world. It will be awesome.

SHARE IT
Christians will one day live with Jesus forever in His perfect kingdom.

▶ *How can you tell your friends about the hope you have for the future with Jesus?*

THE BOTTOM LINE
Amos' message has been a hard one to swallow: everyone who rejects God and lives for themselves will be punished. But those rescued by Jesus have a brilliant future!

PRAY ABOUT IT
Tell God what you think about Him, His plan, and His King (Jesus).

→ TAKE IT FURTHER
For a glimpse of the future, try page 116.

The Trinity — an inconvenient truth?

In each issue of engage we pause a moment to explain a key truth about God, the Bible and Christianity. In ESSENTIAL we gather together all the teaching from the Bible on a particular subject, and try to explain it. We're going to plunge straight in at the deep end by looking at one of the trickiest truths of all — the Trinity.

ONE GOD OR THREE?

The Bible's pretty clear throughout that there is only one God. Right from the start, it tells us that this one God made everything, and the "gods" that the rest of mankind worship are, in fact, nothing at all — fakes.

It's surprising, then, that Christians seem to be talking about three Gods, not one: God the Father, Jesus the Son, and the Holy Spirit. Why is that? Well, because right from the start, it's been obvious that the question of what God is like is far from simple. Take creation, for example. God says "*Let us make...*" (Genesis 1 v 26). And throughout the OT there is talk of *the Spirit of God*, and other references that must have made the Israelites scratch their heads.

And when Jesus comes, it gets more confusing. He says and does stuff that only God can do — raises the dead, calms storms and forgives sins. And He says things that only God can say — even taking the holy, special name of God — I AM — for Himself (John 8 v 58). His claim to be God is what eventually got Him executed (Matthew 26 v 63–65).

It wasn't that God left heaven, and turned into Jesus, and then went back to heaven and turned into the Spirit. No — all three are talked of as God, and are around at the same time. At Jesus' baptism, we read that the **Father's** voice was heard from heaven, and the **Spirit** descended on **Jesus** in the form of a dove (Matthew 3 v 16–17). Later on, Jesus tells us to go and make disciples of all nations, baptising them in the name of the Father, Son and Holy Spirit (Matthew 28 v 19–20).

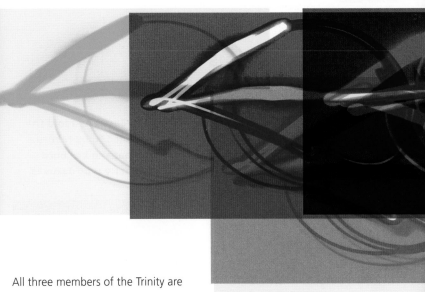

All three members of the Trinity are fully God and have a close, loving relationship with each other. And they share a common mission — to bring us back into a right relationship with themselves. This was ultimately achieved by Jesus dying on the cross in our place. God the Father was behind this perfect plan, and the Holy Spirit is at work in the lives of those who turn to God.

THE BASICS

So how do we sum up what the Bible says about God – the Trinity? How about this…

- ☑ **There is one God...**
- ☑ **made up of three eternal and equal persons.**
- ☑ **They share the same essence and substance (they are the made of the same "stuff")...**
- ☑ **but they are distinct from each other.**

DOES IT REALLY MATTER?

Holding to these difficult truths is what makes us truly Christian — as opposed to Jehovah's Witnesses, Unitarians or Mormons — all of whom say that one or more of these statements is false. Muslims reject the Trinity, saying that Christians worship three Gods — but we need to have confidence that the Trinity is the truth of what God is like.

It might seem a bit "inconvenient" to think of God as a Trinity, but we need to stand firm on it — because it's **the truth**. It's the picture the Bible gives us of what God is really like. It's amazing to realise that at the heart of the universe is, not a proud dictator, but a relationship of unselfish love that is passionate about rescuing lost people like you and me.

42 | John – Signs of life

When we left John's Gospel (day 15), Jesus had told the Jewish leader Nicodemus that he needed to be reborn. Nicodemus hasn't grasped what it means to be "born again". And he hasn't worked out exactly who Jesus is.

◉ Read John 3 v 9–21

ENGAGE YOUR BRAIN

▷ Why is Jesus the best person to answer his questions? (v12–13)

▷ What do you think it means that Jesus will be "lifted up"? (v14)

Jesus reminds Nicodemus of an Old Testament story, when poisonous snakes killed many Israelites (Numbers 21 v 4–9). The people who looked up at a special bronze snake were saved. "That's how being *born again* works" says Jesus. "I will be lifted up (on a cross). People who look up to me, by trusting and believing, will be saved."

▷ Why did God send His Son into the world? (v16–18)

The theme of this section seems to be how people react to Jesus — believing or not believing, loving or hating the light. Fill in the box to show the consequences of these reactions.

Believes	v 18
Doesn't believe	v 18
Hates the light	v 20
Loves the light	v 21

PRAY ABOUT IT

Talk to God about your own response to Jesus. Ask God to help you trust only in Him to be saved. Confess the times when you've loved the darkness more than the light, and ask Him to help you change.

THE BOTTOM LINE

Being born into eternal life comes by turning to Jesus on the cross.

→ TAKE IT FURTHER

Look towards page 117.

43 | The Best Man's speech

Who are the most important people on a wedding day? What things do other people do to focus the attention on the bride and groom?

👁 **Read John 3 v 22–30**

Both Jesus and John the Baptist are baptising people at the same time. The danger arises of a rivalry between them, but John is quick to defuse the situation.

ENGAGE YOUR BRAIN

▶ *What has John always claimed about himself? (v28)*

▶ *How does he describe the connection between himself and Jesus? (v29)*

John says that Jesus is the most important one, like a bridegroom at a wedding. So he's happy to have the job of pointing people to Jesus (v29). John then states a great principle of living life as a Christian — ***"Jesus must become greater, I must become less."*** (v30)

▶ *When are you tempted to be the centre of attention, rather than Christ?*

👁 **Read verses 31–36**

▶ *What is it that sets Jesus apart? (v31, 34, 35)*

Verse 36 repeats some familiar themes in John's Gospel — belief, eternal life and rejection.

PRAY ABOUT IT

Pray again for the people you prayed for on Day 28. Ask God to give you the opportunity to be like John the Baptist and shine the spotlight on Jesus.

THE BOTTOM LINE

Jesus must become greater and we must become less.

➡ **TAKE IT FURTHER**

More from the Best Man's speech on page 117.

44 | Thirst quencher

What's the thirstiest you've ever been? Now think about a desert, the hot sun beating down, no water for miles. Thirsty yet? Go get a drink of water and we'll look at today's Bible bit in three sips.

 Read John 4 v 1–15

Sip 1 – *Where is Jesus? (v5)*
Jews didn't normally associate with Samaritans. History and religion had separated the two races. But Jesus is no ordinary Jew — His mission is for **everybody**.

Sip 2 – *Who does Jesus speak to?*
Jewish men wouldn't usually speak to women. But Jesus is no ordinary man. We find out later that the woman is a bit of a moral outcast (v17–18).

Compare Nicodemus (from two days ago) and the Samaritan woman:

	Nicodemus	Samaritan Woman
Male/female		
Nationality		
Social standing		

The gospel is for everybody. John may have deliberately put these two conversations next to each other to teach us that people from all walks of life need Jesus.

Sip 3 – *What does Jesus offer the woman?*
This is no ordinary drink. Jesus doesn't just offer a quick drink to fix the immediate problem. He offers *living water* to fix the big problem. Jesus' solution to the problem of sin is eternal life.

PRAY ABOUT IT
Jesus doesn't just want to sort out the small problems in our lives. He wants to deal with the big problem of sin. Spend time thanking Jesus for offering us the chance of eternal life.

THE BOTTOM LINE
Jesus offers eternal life to everyone.

➔ TAKE IT FURTHER
Still thirsty? Run to page 117.

45 True worship

Do you know any friends or couples who are impossible to separate? God's word and God's Spirit are an inseparable pair. Today, Jesus teaches us that we need both to truly worship God.

👁 Read John 4 v 16–26

Jesus is still talking to the woman at the well. As Jesus asks about her husband, the woman replies quite defensively, maybe to avoid further difficult questions.

ENGAGE YOUR BRAIN

▶ *What is Jesus' reply? (v17–18)*

▶ *How does this show Jesus' ability to know people deeply?*

Again and again, Jesus shows that He is God. The Samaritan woman recognises Jesus as someone special so she raises the big argument between Jews and Samaritans: *where should you worship God?*

▶ *What time is coming soon? (v21–23)*

▶ *What sort of worshippers will God seek? (v23–25)*

Jesus uses the phrase *"the time is coming"* to point forward to the events of His death and resurrection.

So the argument over worship will be settled by Jesus' death for us all. Then, of course, we won't need to be in a particular place; we can and should worship God anywhere and everywhere.

Jesus also uses the strange phrase *"worship in spirit and in truth"*. When we accept Jesus (*the truth*) into our lives, He gives us His Spirit to help us worship Him in the way we live our lives. Worshipping isn't just singing songs: it's serving God. And that's the whole point of life!

PRAY ABOUT IT

Worship is not just the songs we sing, but the way we live. Ask God to help you worship Him with your whole life.

→ TAKE IT FURTHER

For more, turn to page 117.

46 | Hearing is believing

**What stops you telling people about Jesus?
Do you ever think it's just not the right moment?**

Nothing could stop the Samaritan woman from rushing to tell others about Jesus, even though she wasn't the most popular person in town.

👁 Read John 4 v 27–42

ENGAGE YOUR BRAIN

Three different groups of people react in three different ways to the conversation between the woman and Jesus. What are the different reactions of:

📖 the disciples? (v27, 31–38)

📖 the woman? (v28–30)

📖 the locals? (v39–42)

After their silent surprise at Jesus' companion, the disciples need a lesson in gospel work. Jesus uses food as an example, but the disciples misunderstand the sort of food He's talking about. Jesus explains that while the crop harvest is still four months away, the harvest for people is ready. It's always right to look for opportunities to tell people about Jesus. As proof, John tells us about the amazing reaction of the local people to Jesus.

📖 *What two reasons for believing do the locals have? (v39, 42)*

Some believe because of what the woman told them. Even more believe when Jesus spends two days in the town. Their conclusion? This man really is the Saviour of the world!

PRAY ABOUT IT

Do you believe it's always time to spread the gospel? Tell God about the things that stop you. Ask Him to give you the boldness to tell people about Jesus, as the Samaritan woman did.

THE BOTTOM LINE

It's always time to tell people about Jesus.

→ TAKE IT FURTHER

Hungry for more? Try page 118.

47 | Word's worth

Whose words do you trust without any doubt or question? We're often quick to trust people in authority or close friends and family. But do we always take Jesus at His word?

👁 **Read John 4 v 43–54**

Jesus had recently been in Samaria. People there believed Him after hearing His life-changing words. But in Galilee (Jesus' home area), people wanted to see more and more miracles before they'd believe. They wouldn't take Jesus at His word.

ENGAGE YOUR BRAIN

▷ *Why is the royal official desperate to see Jesus? (v46–47)*

▷ *What is Jesus' criticism? (v48)*

▷ *How does the man respond?*

Jesus' criticism in v48 is probably aimed at everyone in Galilee, not just the official. Jesus knows that just seeing miracles doesn't necessarily mean people will believe that He's God's Son. The official proves that he trusts in Jesus by continuing to ask. Jesus heals his son at exactly that moment (v53).

▷ *What's impressive about the man's reaction? (v50)*

▷ *What is the result for his family and everyone in his house? (v53)*

GET ON WITH IT

Jesus wants people to believe in Him. To believe that He is God's Son.

▷ *Do you believe Jesus' words and claims about Himself?*

▷ *How is this obvious in the way you live?*

PRAY ABOUT IT

Ask God to help you really believe Jesus' words and to let your belief in Jesus affect the way you live.

THE BOTTOM LINE

Take Jesus at His word.

→ **TAKE IT FURTHER**

God's perfect timing — page 118.

48 | New for old

As we look back over chapters 2–4 of John's Gospel, it becomes clear that Jesus has been throwing out the old ways. But far from leaving it at that, Jesus has been replacing the old with the new. The kingdom of God is here and that means CHANGE.

ENGAGE YOUR BRAIN

If you have time, read all of chapters 2–4 again. (If not, read 4 v 21–26) Look out for the big reversals or changes that Jesus makes:

OLD	2 v 19
NEW	2 v 21

OLD	4 v 11-12
NEW	4 v 13-14

OLD	4 v 19-20
NEW	4 v 23

Jesus replaces the old religious way of doing things with the new kingdom way. The old temple is replaced with the new temple, Jesus Himself; the traditional rabbi or teacher (Nicodemus) is taught about new birth into God's kingdom (John 3 v 3–7).

Two more renewals are given in the story of the woman at the well — the old well (Jacob's well) is replaced by Jesus, the living water; and the old worship (in Jerusalem or Gerazim) with the new worship, *"in spirit and truth"*.

When Jesus came to earth and died and rose again, everything changed for ever.

PRAY ABOUT IT

Ask God to continue His work of renewal in your life — throwing out your old sinful ways and living a new life for Him. Spend some time being honest with God about the areas in which you are reluctant to let Him change and rule you.

THE BOTTOM LINE

The old religious ways are gone; Jesus brings in the new.

→ TAKE IT FURTHER

No *Take it further* today, sorry.

49 Get up and go

Ever been in a situation where you had to rely on other people (broken leg, lying sick in bed)? Now try to imagine being unable to walk or help yourself for 38 years!

👁 Read John 5 v 1–15

John gives us some detailed evidence about the location of Jesus' next sign — a pool, surrounded by five colonnades (roofed passageways with lots of columns), near the Sheep Gate (v2). Archaeologists found a pool exactly like this, which assures us that this really is historical fact.

In the report of this miracle, John introduces us to someone whose need is deep and long term.

ENGAGE YOUR BRAIN

▷ *What unusual question does Jesus ask him? (v6)*
▷ *What does Jesus do for him and how? (v8)*

Jesus' question seems strange, but it would mean a huge change of life for the man after 38 years. And he'd probably not be able to get money from begging any more. Once again, Jesus displays His power through a miracle. He doesn't need a "magical" pool, just a few words.

The Jews have already questioned Jesus about His authority (2 v 18). Now they spot the lame man and take him to task for breaking one of the Sabbath rules about work (v10).

▷ *How have they missed the point of Jesus' miraculous sign?*

GET ON WITH IT

Jesus finds the man again to tell him to stop sinning. The *"something worse"* is God's punishment for people who refuse to turn away from their sin. Have you listened to Jesus' warning?

PRAY ABOUT IT

Thank God that even though we can't help ourselves with our sin problem, Jesus can heal us.

THE BOTTOM LINE

Jesus can help all those who can't help themselves.

→ TAKE IT FURTHER

Get up and walk to page 118.

50 Family business

Can you imagine doing the same job as one of your parents? Does it appeal, or does it sound like the saddest thing you could imagine? Today Jesus explains that He is following the family business — giving life.

👁 Read John 5 v 16–18

Yesterday, we saw Jesus heal the paralysed man by the pool. Now the Jews begin to persecute Jesus because He did it on the Sabbath (the Jewish holy day). Jesus explains that God, His Father, is at work, even on the Sabbath. So Jesus works too.

ENGAGE YOUR BRAIN

▶ *Why did this make the Jews even angrier? (v18)*

C.S. Lewis said that you could only come to three conclusions about Jesus' claims to be God's Son — He was either *"mad, bad or God"*. The Jews concluded that Jesus was "bad" because He claimed to be God.

👁 Read verses 19-23

▶ *What jobs does Jesus say He's involved in? (v21–22)*

▶ *What is the purpose of Jesus' work? (v23)*

This passage shows us a little bit about how the Trinity works. Jesus can only do what He sees the Father doing (v19), but the way the Father works is to entrust the work to His Son (v22). It wasn't blasphemy for Jesus to claim to be doing God's work for Him. It's the way that God works. *(For more on the Trinity, p54.)*

THINK IT OVER

Now think about your own reaction to Jesus (*mad, bad or God?*). Does your life give other people a right view of Jesus?

PRAY ABOUT IT

What do your friends say about Jesus? Ask God to help them understand the truth of who Jesus is. Pray for opportunities to talk to them about what Jesus came to do.

THE BOTTOM LINE

Jesus is at work on God's business.

→ TAKE IT FURTHER

For homework, turn to page 118.

51 Waking the dead

Words can be powerful. Maybe you can command your dog to "sit" or "roll over". Some people have the authority to boss people around. But only Jesus' words have the power to change death into life.

👁 Read John 5 v 24–30

Jesus' work is to do what His Father does — to bring life. He does this with His powerful words, just as His words healed the paralysed guy by the pool.

ENGAGE YOUR BRAIN

▶ *What happens to people who believe Jesus' words? (v24)*

▶ *Why do Jesus' words have such power? (v26–27)*

The paralysed man had life restored to his "dead" limbs. That miracle was a picture of what Jesus is now saying. The same power gives eternal life to those who are spiritually dead. Those who turn their backs on their old sinful ways and accept Jesus' offer of forgiveness and new life. And when Jesus returns, the dead will rise from their graves (v28–29)! God the Father gives Jesus all power and authority.

When Jesus returns, the dead will be raised, to face God's judgment. There are two outcomes for those who are raised — eternal life with Jesus or eternal death in hell.

We make that choice while we're still alive — we can choose Jesus and eternal life, or we can choose to live for ourselves on earth and be punished later.

PRAY ABOUT IT

We often think of Jesus as Saviour, Lord or friend but we must not forget He is also the Judge. Talk to God about the choice you've made. Ask Him to help you live for Jesus while you're on earth, so you're ready for when He returns as Judge.

THE BOTTOM LINE

Jesus' power transforms death to life.

➔ TAKE IT FURTHER

For more on Jesus the Judge, try page 118.

52 | Witness for the defence

"You'll never guess who I've just been talking to" says your friend, "only... (insert name of celebrity here)." But how do you know if they're telling the truth? What sort of evidence would you demand?

👁 Read John 5 v 31–40

Jesus is continuing His response to the Jews who want to kill Him for claiming to be God's Son. Where is the evidence to prove that Jesus is who He claims to be?

As if He were putting a court case together, Jesus calls the witnesses in His defence. Jesus mentions three witnesses. Can you identify them?

▣ Witness 1 – verses 33–35
▣ Witness 2 – verse 36
▣ Witness 3 – verses 37–40

John the Baptist shone the spotlight on Jesus; Jesus' miracles are even clearer evidence; and God's own word is the best evidence of all. The Old Testament pointed to Jesus, and Jesus made many Old Testament prophecies come true. But the Jews still refused to believe it.

ENGAGE YOUR BRAIN

▣ What have the Jews missed in their study of the Scriptures?

▣ What's the consequence of this? (v40)

👁 Read verses 41-47

The problem was that these people looked for praise in the wrong places (v44). Their study of the Old Testament didn't lead to obedience to God! Moses was their hero, yet they failed to realise that he had pointed to Jesus as their Rescuer.

PRAY ABOUT IT

We have the same evidence in the Bible. And we can read about Jesus' life, His words and His miracles in the New Testament. Ask God to help you learn more about Jesus through His word. Pray God will open the eyes of your non-Christian friends to see Christ in the Bible and believe in Him.

THE BOTTOM LINE

The whole Bible is our evidence pointing to Jesus Christ.

→ TAKE IT FURTHER

More evidence on page 119.

53 | Genesis – In the beginning

Have you ever watched those TV shows where they start with a recap by Voiceover Man and his big booming voice: "Previously on …" Well, verses 1–3 of chapter 5 remind us of the story so far in Genesis.

👁 Read Genesis 5 v 1-3

ENGAGE YOUR BRAIN

▶ *Verses 1–2 sound great but what is the problem with Seth? (v3)*

▶ *Whose likeness was Adam made in (v1)?*

▶ *What is the problem with being like Adam rather than like God?*

Have a read through the whole section, verses 1–32.

▶ *Which phrase is repeated again and again?*

▶ *Are there any exceptions to this?*

▶ *What's different about this person? (v21–24)*

"And then he died". Despite the amazing lifespans — check out Methuselah — God's judgment on Adam and his family still holds. They all die eventually. We're still looking for the descendant who will crush the serpent's head (Genesis 3 v 15).

SHARE IT

Death. They call it "the ultimate statistic": 1 in 1 will die. But not Enoch, and there are a couple of other exceptions in the Bible too. Why not chat about it to a friend today? *Are they frightened of death? What would happen if everyone lived for ever? Do they believe in life after death? Why / why not?*

PRAY ABOUT IT

We know from the rest of the Bible that this life is not all there is. All humans die once and face God's judgment. Pray for people you know who are not trusting in Christ. Pray that they would before it's too late.

THE BOTTOM LINE

Death is not the end.
Good news for some…

→ TAKE IT FURTHER

It's the end of this page.
For the after-page, go to 119.

54 | Grieving God

Andrew means "brave", Sophie means "wisdom". Kevin means "beautiful at birth". Look back at Genesis 5 v 28-29. Was Noah's dad just being optimistic when he named him? Will he bring comfort from the curse? Let's find out...

👁 Read Genesis 6 v 1–4

So the population is increasing, but they're still sinning and God's judgment (as we saw yesterday) is still in place. Some Bible experts think the 120-year limit refers to the amount of time they have left before the flood. Others think God was reducing people's lifespan.

And don't worry too much about the identity of the *"sons of God"*. They might be angels, might not. What is clear is that they were disobeying God.

👁 Read verses 5–8

ENGAGE YOUR BRAIN

▷ *How bad have things got?*

▷ *What reaction(s) does God have?*

▷ *Is there any glimmer of hope? (v8)*

Have you ever made something that took a lot of care and hours of work? A painting, sculpture, design project or model? How wrong would it have to go before you destroyed it or threw it away?

The world had become very different from God's very good creation (Genesis chapter 1). Though nothing had happened outside of His control, God was still grieved and troubled by the evil and ruin He saw.

PRAY ABOUT IT

Have you ever thought that your sin *"grieves God to the heart"*? Spend some time saying sorry to Him.

THE BOTTOM LINE

Our sin pains and offends God.

→ TAKE IT FURTHER

Check out page 119.

55 Ark and ride

Have you ever seen one of those enormous cruise ships? They look like five floating football stadiums in one. Well, the ark was pretty big — but it wasn't a cruise ship. It was a lifeboat.

👁 **Read Genesis 6 v 8–10**

ENGAGE YOUR BRAIN

▶ What is special about Noah?

▶ OK, that was a trick question! Who decides Noah will be special? (v8)

👁 **Read verses 11–22**

▶ What is the problem with the earth? (v11–12)

▶ How exactly is God going to deal with it? (v13)

We often think God's judgment is unfair—an overreaction maybe — but take another look at v5 and v11–12.

TALK IT THROUGH

Chat to another Christian about God's judgment. Do you find it difficult to understand? Does it seem fair? Why does it matter that God can't ignore evil? How does the cross show how seriously He takes sin?

Noah wasn't anything special in himself, but God chose him to be rescued.

▶ What was God's wild rescue plan for Noah? (v13–21)

▶ List some of the ways in which God shows His mercy in this passage. Jot them down here:

PRAY ABOUT IT

None of us deserves to be saved by God. We're just as wicked as the next person, but God has always been the God of rescue. Can you think of any other examples of God rescuing His people? Thank God for them.

➡ **TAKE IT FURTHER**

Swim along to page 119.

56 Flood warning

If you've ever seen a flood on TV, you'll know how destructive loads of water can be. But the flood in Genesis was seriously devastating — every living thing on the face of the earth was destroyed.

 Read Genesis 7 v 1–24

ENGAGE YOUR BRAIN

▷ *Jot down the basic order of events:*

_____

_____

_____

_____

▷ *Why do Noah and family escape?*
▷ *Why do you think Noah has to take more of some animals than others? Think about it!*
▷ *Who shuts the door of the ark? (v16) What does that show us?*
▷ *Remember the pattern of sin, judgment and mercy we've been seeing since Genesis 3? Fill in the table for chapters 6 and 7:*

Sin?	
God's judgment?	
God's mercy?	

GET ON WITH IT
"And Noah did all that the Lord commanded him". If you've ever seen footage of a rescue team at work up a mountain or at sea, you'll know that the people being rescued have to do exactly what they're told. If someone threw you a rope when you were drowning and told you to take hold of it, you'd be pretty stupid to argue. Jesus is our lifeboat — have you accepted that? The alternative is just as terrifying as verses 21–23.

THE BOTTOM LINE
Will you get into the lifeboat before it's too late?

TAKE IT FURTHER
Paddle over to page 119.

57 | Home and dry

Look back at the end of chapter 7 for a minute. "Only Noah was left, and those that were with him in the ark." Pretty scary, being the only living creatures left.

Chapter 8 starts with the words *"But God..."* — probably one of the best phrases in the Bible!

👁 **Read Genesis 8 v 1–14**

ENGAGE YOUR BRAIN

▷ *What happens to halt God's terrifying judgment?*

▷ *What does this tell us about God?*

▷ *What did God make happen to stop the flood? (v1–2)*

▷ *What does this tell us about Him? Any ideas?*

People remember the whole 40 days and 40 nights of rainfall but it took nearly a whole year before the earth was dry enough to stand on again.

▷ *What was Noah's nifty way of checking whether it was safe to disembark from the ark?*

Noah sent a dove to see if there was dry land or not. God had flooded the earth to wash away all the sin and evil. *"But God remembered Noah."* He remembered that Noah had obeyed Him, and He rescued Noah and blessed him loads (more on that in the next few days).

God is in total control of the world, and He cares for everyone and every thing that lives in His world.

PRAY ABOUT IT

Thank God that He cares about you. Thank Him that He is powerful enough to help you, and rescue you from sin. Two very good reasons to pray.

THE BOTTOM LINE

But God remembered Noah.

➔ **TAKE IT FURTHER**

No *Take it further* today.

58 | A fresh start

So all the wicked have been swept away by the flood. The earth is clean. Time for a fresh start?

👁 **Read Genesis 8 v 15–22**

ENGAGE YOUR BRAIN

▷ Who makes the decision to disembark? (v15–16)

▷ How do you think Noah felt to be on dry land again?

▷ What is Noah's first act on dry land? (v20)

▷ What does this show?

▷ How does God react? (v21–22)

Another command to be fruitful and multiply (v17) and no further curse on the ground (v21). Perhaps things are looking up. So has anything changed? Are human beings better? Well, no. Their hearts are still inclined to do evil right from the start (v21).

Yes, that means your heart too. But no more world-destroying floods, not like the last one, even though we deserve to be punished.

Do you believe that your heart is naturally inclined to do evil? Or do you think you're basically a good person? If you're a Christian, you know the answer is the first one. We all do wrong stuff. But God sent Jesus so that we can be forgiven.

SHARE IT

Do your friends recognise the fact that we are **ALL** capable of evil, not just a few criminals? That we all do wrong? It's a truth everyone needs to understand — that we're all sinful and need God's forgiveness.

THE BOTTOM LINE

God loves us *despite* the way we live, not *because* of it.

➡ **TAKE IT FURTHER**

Check out page 119.

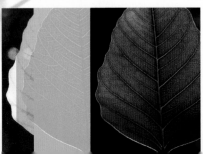

59 | Lifeblood

"God bless ya!" People often say that simple phrase without really knowing what it means. Noah knew — he received God's blessing. God was doing business with him and his family. Let's look at the deal.

👁 **Read Genesis 9 v 1–7**

ENGAGE YOUR BRAIN

▷ *List the ways God blesses Noah and his family:*

▷ *What is Noah warned against doing? (v4)*
▷ *Why is that?*
▷ *Who will be held to account for the spilling of human blood? (v5–6) Any surprises?*

In the Bible, blood = life. Here God is reinforcing just how valuable human life is. Whether another human or even an animal killed someone, then their life would be taken in return.

▷ *What reason does God give for placing such a high value on human life? (v6)*

TALK IT THROUGH

Christians have different views about what the punishment for murder should be. How do you think v6 applies today, if at all? Does the New Testament change anything?

We may not think that v5–6 applies to us. We're not murderers, surely? But Jesus says that being angry with another person is just as bad (Matthew 5 v 21–22). God will hold us all responsible for our actions. But we're not the ones to dish out the punishment — Jesus will do that when He returns.

PRAY ABOUT IT

Thank God that He's given us the world to look after and enjoy. Ask Him to help you treat other people better, as they're made in His image.

THE BOTTOM LINE
Human life is valuable.

➡ **TAKE IT FURTHER**
For a little more, turn to page 120.

60 | Promises promises

What do a wedding ring, an IOU and a rainbow all have in common? Any ideas? Well, they're all things that represent a promise.

Read Genesis 9 v 8–17

ENGAGE YOUR BRAIN

▷ *What does God promise?*

▷ *Who is God's covenant agreement with? (v8–10, 17)*

▷ *How long will it last? (v12, 16)*

▷ *What sign does God give to show He will remember His promise?*

The flood was a huge event. Just in case people were frightened it might happen again, God chose a sign which occurs naturally at the same time as wet weather, to reassure the world of His promise.

▷ *Can you think of any other examples of God keeping His promises in the Bible? Jot down as many as you can think of:*

PRAY ABOUT IT

Thank God for His covenant, because it's a promise for you too. Thank God that He cares about all that He has made. Pick one of God's great promises and spend time thanking Him for it.

THE BOTTOM LINE

God keeps His promises.

→ TAKE IT FURTHER

on page 120 for another reminder of one of God's great promises.

61 Drunk and disorderly

Things are looking good for Noah. Time for a celebratory drink? Or ten? Bottoms up! Don't take that too literally, Noah …

👁 **Read Genesis 9 v 18–23**

ENGAGE YOUR BRAIN

▷ *Try to sum up Noah's behaviour in v21 in one word.*

▷ *What's so bad about Ham's behaviour?*

▷ *What is good about Shem and Japheth's response?*

Not only does Noah have a few too many and make a fool of himself, but Ham decides to have a laugh at his dad's expense and broadcast his drunkenness. Neither of them acts in a way that honours God.

GET ON WITH IT

God says we should honour our parents and treat them with respect (Exodus 20 v 12).

▷ *Do you?*

▷ *How can you show that today/ tomorrow?*

For more on the alcohol issue, check out TAKE IT FURTHER on page 120.

👁 **Read verses 24–29**

ENGAGE YOUR BRAIN

▷ *What is Noah's hung-over reaction?*

▷ *Have we found our serpent-crusher yet? (v29)*

An ugly tale and a sad end. So Noah's definitely not the serpent-crusher. However, he announces God's blessing on two of his sons (v26–27) and God's punishment on the other (v24). Then he dies. The story of God and His people goes on.

THE BOTTOM LINE

Does your behaviour honour God?

→ TAKE IT FURTHER

Stagger over to page 120.

62 | History shaper

So Ham, Shem, Japheth — the world's your oyster...
sorry, you've probably had enough of sea creatures
for a while... So, H, S, and J — where are you gonna go?

👁 Read Genesis 10 v 1–32

Some of Shem's descendants eventually became God's people Israel, and their relationships with the nations around them (Ham and Japheth's descendants) were influenced by the judgment and blessings Noah handed out to his sons in Genesis 9 v 25–27 (Ham's descendants would be slaves to the descendants of Shem and Japheth).

ENGAGE YOUR BRAIN

▷ *Check out Ham's descendants (v6–20). Can you spot any future enemies of Israel?*

We get a little taste of some of the events to come in the rest of the Old Testament here — Egypt, Nineveh, Babylon and the evil cities of Sodom and Gomorrah. All places and people who would have an impact on God's people over the years.

None of this happened by accident. God knows exactly what's going on. All of this shows us how, from the very beginning, God is in control of history. Amazing.

PRAY ABOUT IT

God is in control of the whole world. Pray about countries and places that really need prayer today. Here are a few suggestions for you to research on the internet: Somalia, China, Mexico, Syria.

THE BOTTOM LINE

God is in control of history.

63 | Babel babble

If you could build anything at all (given endless time and resources), what would you build? I bet your project isn't as ambitious as this one...

👁 Read Genesis 11 v 1–9

ENGAGE YOUR BRAIN

▶ What is the motivation behind this project? (v4)

▶ Where have we seen this attitude before?

What's your greatest ambition — to win a reality TV show? To get signed as a professional footballer? To get straight "A"s in all your exams? If so, maybe you're interested in "making a name for yourself". What do you spend time thinking and dreaming about? Does it make God look good? Or just yourself?

▶ What is God's response to Project Babel?

▶ Why do you think God stops them achieving their ambition? Is He just trying to spoil their fun?

Think for a minute about what might happen if human beings could do whatever they wanted with no restrictions (v6). What would the world look like (bearing in mind that people are naturally sinful and greedy)? You want something? Just take it. If someone's in your way, step on them. You don't like someone? Shoot them.

PRAY ABOUT IT

Thank God that He has given us a conscience plus laws and governments which, most of the time, keep us from the chaos of everyone going their own way (Romans 13 v 1–4).

GET ON WITH IT

The Lord's Prayer says: *"Hallowed* (honoured) *be your name"*. How can you honour God's name, rather than your own, today? Think of something practical you can do!

➡ TAKE IT FURTHER

Babble on to Babylon... page 120.

64 | Man hunt

Uh-oh. It's another one of those lists of names, or "genealogies" if you're being clever. So is this bit of the Bible about as interesting as reading the phone book, or is there more to it?

👁 Read Genesis 11 v 10–32

ENGAGE YOUR BRAIN

▶ *Any signs that the serpent-crusher might be on his way?*

God's death sentence on mankind is still going. We've seen that despite the hopeful signs, Noah wasn't the serpent-crusher. But what about this next guy, Abram?

▶ *What facts do we learn about Abram?*

◇

◇

◇

◇

◇

Keep those in mind — they'll be significant later. We're standing on

the edge of Abram's adventures with God — it's going to be awesome. But for now, look back at all you've learned in Genesis so far...

▶ *What have you learned about God?*

▶ *What have you learned about human beings?*

▶ *What have you learned about yourself?*

PRAY ABOUT IT

You know what to do.

THE BOTTOM LINE

God has a perfect plan.

Colossians

Life to the max

Colin is a great guitarist. He's been practicing enthusiastically for hours every day for the last four years, and you can tell. But Sian's not so sure. She says to be a proper guitarist you need to have the right look, wear black all the time, know EVERY Jimi Hendrix riff and hang out with the right people. Following these simple rules, he can be a true guitarist. Colin thought he already was one!

The year is 60AD and the church in Colosse (in what is now Turkey) is packed with new Christians. They're full of enthusiasm for the message of Jesus, but people have been telling them that's not enough. *"Follow these rules and have these experiences if you want to be a true Christian." "Believing in Jesus is one thing, but to know God deeply and please Him fully you need something more."*

Heard anyone say stuff like that? The young Christians in Colosse had, and it sounded attractive. In his letter to the Colossian Christians, Paul says: "HOLD ON GUYS! You don't need anything more to be a Christian; Christ is all you need." A life based on faith in Jesus is the key for a full Christian life. That's the simple message of Colossians.

Paul's letter is a great read if you're a new-ish believer, as it's jammed with the truth of what it really means to be a Christian. And if you've been a believer a bit longer, Colossians is a great refresher course, spurring you on in the Christian life.

65 How to grow a Christian

How would you introduce yourself? How would you describe yourself in an email or letter to someone you've never actually met? Paul introduces himself as an apostle, someone sent by God to tell people about Jesus.

Read Colossians 1 v 1–4

ENGAGE YOUR BRAIN

▶ *How does Paul describe the Christians in Colosse? (v2–4)*

They display the characteristics of growing Christians. They are…

- **Holy (v2)** — set apart for God
- **Faithful (v2)** — serving God, letting their faith in Jesus shine through their lives (v4)
- **Loving (v4)** —they showed great love for other believers (if you're a Christian, you're a *saint*!).

Read verses 5–8

▶ *Where did their faith and love spring from? (v5)*

They trusted God and loved other people because they were sure that their sins were forgiven through Jesus. They had a sure hope that they'd live with God for ever. This changed the way they looked at life — no longer grabbing the best

for themselves, but living for God now, and serving Him, knowing that heaven was a sure thing.

▶ *How should the hope of eternal life affect the way you live?*

The *gospel* is the great news that Jesus died in the place of sinners, so that they could have their sins forgiven. This great news was *"bearing fruit"* all over the world (v6) — many people were becoming Christians. The gospel was spreading, just as it had in Colosse since Epaphras first told them about Jesus (v7).

PRAY ABOUT IT

Ask God to help you grow as a Christian and become more holy, faithful and loving. Where do you want to see the gospel spreading and bearing fruit? Talk to God about it.

→ **TAKE IT FURTHER**

Spring over to page 120.

66 | The knowledge

Before an exam, we cram our heads full of knowledge. Why? So we can answer the questions in the exam and pass it. Well, that's the theory anyway.

👁 **Read Colossians 1 v 9–11**

ENGAGE YOUR BRAIN

▶ *What has Paul been praying for the Christians in Colosse? (v9)*

▶ *Why? (v10)*

▶ *So how does God want His people to live? (v10–11)*

What a great thing to pray — that these guys will know what God wants of them so they can live lives that please Him.

God wants us to bear fruit by serving Him in what we do; constantly learning from God; showing endurance and patience when we're given a hard time for living God's way. But it's not down to us — God gives us the strength to do it (v11).

👁 **Read verses 12–14**

▶ *What excites you most in these verses?*

Christians are God's children. They'll inherit eternal life with God. He's rescued them from sin *(the dominion of darkness)* so that they can live with Him for ever, totally forgiven for all their sins. Pretty amazing stuff, eh?

Read v12–14 again, changing *"you"* and *"us"* to *"me"*. If we're Christians, Jesus has qualified us for eternal life and nothing can change that!

PRAY ABOUT IT

Pray v9–11 for your friends. And then for yourself. And thank God for the great inheritance Christians receive — forgiveness and eternal life with Him!

THE BOTTOM LINE

God rescues His children from darkness and helps them to live lives that please Him.

➔ **TAKE IT FURTHER**

Want more *knowledge*? Try page 120.

67 Numero uno

Who is the number one athlete in the world? Number one fashion designer? Number one influence in your life? Paul wants to tell us who's really number one...

👁 Read Colossians 1 v 15–17

ENGAGE YOUR BRAIN

▷ *Paul is talking about Jesus. How does Paul describe Him in v15?*

▷ *Does anything surprise you in v16–17?*

In Bible times, the son who was born first got special rights and privileges. He was number one. Jesus is in charge of the whole of creation! He is the Creator of all things and everything was created for Him (v16). He's the one who holds the world together (v17)! Jesus is number one.

👁 Read verses 18–20

Jesus is number one in the church — head of all God's people, Christians (v18). Jesus became human but He was fully God (v19).

▷ *Despite being God, what was Jesus prepared to do? (v20)*

Jesus lived as a human so that He could die on the cross in our place and be raised back to life (v18). It was the only way to make it possible for us to be at peace with God.

People were telling the Colossian Christians they needed to do more than just believe in Jesus and be forgiven by Him. That's just not true! Jesus is enough, because He is Lord of everything. If you have Jesus, you've already got everything!

PRAY ABOUT IT

Read through the verses again, remembering who Jesus really is, thanking Him for all He's done.

THE BOTTOM LINE

Jesus is number one. Jesus makes it possible to be at peace with God.

→ TAKE IT FURTHER

For more on number one, turn to page number 121.

68 | Before and after

Seen those before and after ads? BEFORE: someone chubby photographed in terrible light, from a bad angle, looking miserable. AFTER: they look half the weight (and just happen to be in great light, in great clothes and smiling!).

Yesterday, Paul told us that Jesus is number one. He is all we need to make peace with God. Now Paul shows us the Christian's BEFORE and AFTER pictures.

👁 **Read Colossians 1 v 21–23**

ENGAGE YOUR BRAIN

▸ *Before people become Christians, what's their relationship with God like? (v21)*

▸ *After having their lives turned around by Jesus, how does God now see them? (v22)*

Before someone becomes a Christian, they're an enemy of God. This is obvious from the way they disobey Him in their thoughts and actions (v21). But Jesus gave His body in death on the cross to take the punishment we deserve. If we trust in His death to put us right with God, then God sees us as holy and without guilt. Squeaky clean!

▸ *So what should Christians do in response to what Jesus has done for them? (v23)*

GET ON WITH IT

▸ *What specific things in your life do you need to change in response to what Jesus has done for you?*

▸ *How can you make it more obvious that you are an AFTER, not a BEFORE?*

THE BOTTOM LINE

Fill it in yourself today. In less than 10 words, summarise what God has taught you today. Then pray about it.

➔ TAKE IT FURTHER

Before you go, check out the AFTERthought on page 121.

69 | Solving the mystery

People were telling Christians in Colosse that they needed to understand secret and mysterious things to be true believers. But Paul says that's rubbish; you just need Jesus. So why is Paul now talking about a mystery???

👁 Read Colossians 1 v 24–27

Paul had suffered a lot for telling people about Jesus. In fact, he was writing this letter from prison. But He was happy to suffer for Jesus and for God's people (v24).

ENGAGE YOUR BRAIN

▶ *Paul describes the word of God as a mystery that had been hidden for ages. But did God keep it a mystery? (v26–27)*

Brilliantly, God chose to reveal the truth to people like these Christians in Colosse. Ordinary people like us!

Jesus Christ is the answer to this mystery (v27). For centuries, God had promised to rescue His people. He did it through Jesus! The mysterious treasure we all need is actually Jesus in our lives.

👁 Read verses 28–29

▶ *What did Paul work hard at, which we must work hard at too? (v28)*

See, it's no mystery at all! Everyone needs Jesus. God doesn't keep it a secret. He wants us to work hard at telling everyone about Jesus and what He has done. And Jesus gives us the energy to do it! (v29)

PRAY ABOUT IT

Thank God for revealing the truth to you. Ask Him to give you the strength and opportunities to tell others the amazing truth about Jesus.

THE BOTTOM LINE

God has revealed the mystery to us — that Jesus is the only way to have our sins forgiven.

→ TAKE IT FURTHER

Nothing mysterious about the *Take It Further* section; it's on page 121.

70 | What's the secret?

**What's the secret to a successful relationship?
What's the secret to passing exams? What's the
secret ingredient that makes chocolate so yummy?
What's the secret to knowing God?**

Read Colossians 2 v 1–5

ENGAGE YOUR BRAIN

▷ *What does Paul want for the
Christians in Colosse? (v2)*

▷ *Do you ever pray these things
for Christians you know?*

Paul says his purpose is for them to
be encouraged, united, showing love
for each other, and he wants them
to know Jesus. Paul was prepared to
work hard and go through all kinds
of struggles for this. Do you want the
same things for yourself and for your
friends that Paul wanted for these
Christians?

▷ *So what's the secret to knowing
God? (v2–3)*

Sorry, trick question! There is no
secret! You don't need any secret
knowledge or need to do anything
weird or have special abilities. You
just need Jesus. All the treasures of
God are found in Jesus!

Read verses 6–7

Paul says: You've started well
following Jesus — now stick at it!

▷ *How are Christians encouraged
to live?*

As Christians grow, they need to
continue living Jesus' way, building
their lives on Him, becoming strong
in their faith. Jesus gives Christians
everything they need. He saved them
from their sins. He's given them the
Bible to teach them, and the Holy
Spirit to help them live for Him!
So they should be bursting with
thankfulness (v7)!

PRAY ABOUT IT

Thank Jesus that He's all you need.
Take some extra time now to thank
Him for what He's done in your life.

→ TAKE IT FURTHER

It's no secret... go to page 121.

71

Cut it out!

Some food packaging is designed to look as if there's more food in it than there really is. Like a nice big bag of nachos that actually contains about three of them. Annoying, eh?

Paul warns us about people whose ideas about life promise a lot, but are really just hollow and empty.

👁 Read Colossians 2 v 8–10

ENGAGE YOUR BRAIN

▷ *Paul says watch out for teaching that relies on* **what** *rather than* **what**? *(v8)*

We're bombarded with attractive ideas all the time. A lot of them have great principles involved (save the planet, end poverty, be a better person) but if they're based on human traditions and not on Jesus, then they're not the real deal. First and foremost, Christians live for Jesus. He's the basis of our lives, not man-made traditions and ideals.

👁 Read verses 11–12

Uh-oh, Paul mentions circumcision. Don't worry guys, he's not saying we have to cut off bits of our wotnots!

▷ *What does Paul say Christians cut off (or "put off") from their lives? (v11)*

In Old Testament times, circumcision was a sign of belonging to God. For Christians, cutting off our old sinful ways is a sign of belonging to God.

Paul says that when people become Christians, they're both buried with Jesus and raised with Him. Christians have *buried* their old sinful way of living and are *raised* to a new life with Jesus!

GET ON WITH IT

▷ *What sins do you need to cut out from your life?*

Talk to the Lord about it.

THE BOTTOM LINE

Cut out sins from your life.

→ TAKE IT FURTHER

Make the cut... page 121.

72 | Nailing the truth

**Paul now reminds Christians exactly what
God has done for them through His Son, Jesus.
Listen up, because this applies to YOU.**

👁 Read Colossians 2 v 13–15

ENGAGE YOUR BRAIN

▷ *How does Paul describe
Christians before they're
rescued by Jesus (v13)?*

Before turning to Jesus, people are as
good as *dead* — separated from God
by their sins against Him. But when
God forgives their sins, He makes
them *alive* again, bringing them back
to Him, giving them new life.

▷ *What does Paul say was
cancelled when Jesus died
on the cross? (v14)*

▷ *What else has God done for
His people, Christians? (v15)*

The *"written code"* (or *"charges"* or
"legal indebtedness") means the debt
we owe God. It's like a bill showing
the huge debt we owe God for our
sins against Him. We've treated God
so badly that it's a debt we could
never pay. But by His death in our

place, Jesus has nailed our debts
to the cross, paying them for us.

By trusting in Jesus' death on our
behalf, all our sins are forgiven (v13).
Wiped out for ever! God has rescued
His people from the powers of evil.
When Jesus died and was raised back
to life, God publicly defeated death,
sin and evil powers (Satan). God's
people are rescued from the sin that
had control of their lives.

PRAY ABOUT IT
Read today's verses again and tell
God how it makes you feel.

THE BOTTOM LINE
Through Jesus' death on the cross,
God has forgiven Christians' sins and
rescued them from the grip of evil.

→ TAKE IT FURTHER
Hammer it in a bit deeper: page 121.

73 Chasing shadows

Laura has a photo of her boyfriend, Tom, in her purse, which she looks at all the time. But when Tom's with her, she doesn't look at the photo at all. Why waste your time with a picture when you have the real thing?

Read Colossians 2 v 16–17

ENGAGE YOUR BRAIN

▷ *What were the Christians in Colosse being judged about?*

People were telling them that they had to follow loads of rules to be right with God. But these Old Testament laws pointed to **Jesus** coming to save His people. Now that Jesus is here, He's the only way to be forgiven. Keeping these rules just isn't enough. Don't settle for the shadow when you've got the real thing in Jesus (v17)!

Read verses 18–23

▷ *What's the biggest mistake made by people who say you need to obey certain rules to be a Christian? (v19)*

▷ *Who is the head of God's people ("the body")?*

If anyone says you need to follow certain rules or have certain experiences for a full Christian life, they've missed the point. Jesus is enough. Yes, we want to obey God's commands, but it's only Jesus' death that brings us forgiveness.

TALK IT THROUGH

What do people sometimes say we need as well as Jesus? What rules and traditions can get in the way of living for Jesus? Why not talk about these things with Christian friends.

THE BOTTOM LINE

Trying to keep rules won't put you right with God. Only trusting Jesus to forgive you leads to a full Christian life.

PRAY ABOUT IT

You're on your own today. There must be loads of things to talk to God about.

→ TAKE IT FURTHER

Chase the shadows to page 121.

74 Back to the future

Paul's been explaining the truth about Christianity: it's all about Jesus. That's the theory; now he moves on to the practice — how to live as a Christian.

👁 Read Colossians 3 v 1–4

Paul tells us what's happened to Christians in the *past*, what's true for them in the *present*, and what will happen in the *future*.

THE PAST

Christians have died to their old way of life and have been raised with Jesus to live for Him and with Him.

THE PRESENT
🅳 *What is true for Christians right now? (v3)*

If you're a Christian, Jesus died for YOU. You're one of His people now, and your life is kept safe ("*hidden*") with Him in heaven. Your future with God is safe!

THE FUTURE

When Jesus returns, Christians will be revealed to be God's children. They'll be like Jesus!

🅳 *So what should Christians be doing now? (v2)*

GET ON WITH IT

We shouldn't get bogged down with our everyday lives, as if that's all there is. We must live our lives for Jesus, remembering that we'll live with Him for ever, becoming more like Him.

🅳 *How can you "set your heart on things above"?*

🅳 *How can you focus your thoughts on better things?*

PRAY ABOUT IT

Thank God for the past, present and future Christian life. Thank Him that your future is safe with Jesus!

THE BOTTOM LINE

If you're a Christian, your past, present and future are safe with Christ. Our eyes should be fixed on a glorious future with Jesus.

➡ TAKE IT FURTHER

Find the future on page 122.

75 Get it sorted

Oi! Sort your life out! That's what Paul said to the Colossians (well, sort of) and it's what God is saying to us...

👁 Read Colossians 3 v 5–11

ENGAGE YOUR BRAIN

▷ *What kinds of things do we need to throw out of our lives? (v5, v8–9)*

▷ *What is God's reaction to sin? (v6)*

▷ *Why should we be fighting the sin in our lives? (v9–10)*

God hates sin; He won't stand for it and will punish those who sin against Him (v6). But Christians have had *all* their sins forgiven by God, so they want to please Him by throwing out sin from their lives.

It's a real struggle, but God helps us do it, helping us become more and more like Him (v10). This is true for all Christians, no matter who they are or where they're from (v11)!

GET ON WITH IT

Look again at verses 5, 8 and 9. Grab some paper and make a list of *specific* sins you need to kick out of your life. Be brutally honest with yourself.

PRAY ABOUT IT

Spend time bringing these things to God in prayer.

TALK IT THROUGH

We all have sin issues we need to deal with. It's often easier if we have someone we're accountable to. Pluck up the courage to talk to an older Christian about the stuff you really struggle with. They can pray with you and encourage you.

THE BOTTOM LINE

Don't delay. Tackle that sin.

→ TAKE IT FURTHER

Joined-up thinking on page 122.

76

Holy wardrobe

Is there a common "Christian look"?
Is the equation SOCK + SANDALS = CHRISTIAN true?
Does it matter what Christians wear?
Paul says that it does...

◉ **Read Colossians 3 v 12–14**

ENGAGE YOUR BRAIN

Christians are God's own people. They are holy, set apart to serve Him. And God loves them massively! OK, so Paul doesn't tell us where to go shopping, but he does tell us the characteristics Christians should clothe themselves in.

▷ *Below, list the 7 qualities we should wear (v12–14):*

-
-
-
-
-
-
-

▷ *Which ones do you struggle with?*

▷ *What's the motive for us to forgive other people? (v13)*

▷ *What's the key ingredient to all of these good qualities? (v14)*

For Christians, God has forgiven all their disobedience and sins against Him, so they should show the same forgiveness when people wrong them (v13). Just as our love for others (even those people who get on our nerves) should be motivated by God's endless love for us (v12).

GET ON WITH IT

On spare paper, list two people you get on with and two you don't. Make them a mix of ages. Next to each one, write down how you can actively show one of the 7 qualities to them.

PRAY ABOUT IT

Thank God that He loves you so ridiculously much! Ask Him to help you do the stuff you scribbled down.

THE BOTTOM LINE

Out of love for God, Christians long to live in a way that's pleasing to Him.

➡ **TAKE IT FURTHER**

More love stuff on page 122.

77 | Body language

Christians are perfect. They're always loving, helpful and encouraging. Christians always get along brilliantly together and never argue, right? You don't look convinced!

OK, maybe we struggle with each other sometimes. Here are Paul's tips for getting along with other Christians…

👁 TIP 1 Read Colossians 3 v 15

▷ *How are Christians described?*

▷ *So how should we act towards other Christians?*

All Christians are part of the same *"body"*, with Jesus as our head. He's forgiven our sins and made us at peace with God. So He expects us to act in peace and kindness towards other believers. Well, it makes sense, doesn't it?

👁 TIP 2 – Read verse 16

"The word of Christ" — the awesome message of what Jesus has done for us — should be at the centre of our lives. We need to study the Bible together, teaching each other from God's word, and singing praise songs to God together, thanking Him for all He's done.

👁 TIP 3 – Read verse 17

▷ *What command is repeated in each of verses 15, 16 and 17?*

Are you grateful to God for what He's done in your life? Christians show their gratitude to God by living their **whole lives** for Him. Everything we do and say should be done and said for Jesus. What a challenge!

GET ON WITH IT

▷ *How can you get on more peacefully with "difficult" Christians you know?*

▷ *Are you reading the Bible together with other Christians?*

▷ *Who could you start reading God's word with?*

PRAY ABOUT IT

Pray about your response to the *Get on with it* section.

→ TAKE IT FURTHER

More body language on page 122.

78 Family fortunes

Someone once said: "Life would be easy if it wasn't for other people." Actually, I said it. But it's true, our relationships can be a cause of real difficulty sometimes. They're HARD WORK!

Yesterday we read: *"Whatever you do… do it all in the name of the Lord Jesus"*. Paul says we must serve God in our relationships. Today we'll look at two of those relationships …

👁 Read Colossians 3 v 18–19

ENGAGE YOUR BRAIN
▷ *What do you think v18 means?*

▷ *And what responsibility do husbands have? (v19)*

This is a really tricky subject that people can get upset about. So if you're starting to fume, go straight to the **Take it further** section to delve into it. But since most of us aren't married yet, let's look at a relationship a little closer to home…

👁 Read verses 20–21

▷ *How much should we obey our parents? Why?*

▷ *And what's the news for fathers?*

Did you get that? We must obey our parents in *everything*!

OK, obviously not if they're going against God's commands, but in everything else we must obey them because it *pleases the Lord*. Yes, it's really hard sometimes, but what better reason to honour our parents. We do it out of love for God.

GET ON WITH IT
▷ *How can you obey your parents more? What do you need to work really hard on?*

PRAY ABOUT IT
Talk to God about any issues raised today. Ask Him to give you clear guidance, and to help you serve Him in your relationships.

→ TAKE IT FURTHER
Go and tidy your room! Or, failing that, take it further on page 122.

79 Working class

What's your attitude towards work (school work, a job you have, chores around the house)? Do you plod along grudgingly or throw yourself into it wholeheartedly?

👁 Read Colossians 3 v 22–4 v 1

Back when Paul was writing, rich people had slaves working in their homes. But Paul's advice is relevant for any kind of work we do.

ENGAGE YOUR BRAIN

▷ *What should a Christian's attitude be towards their boss or teachers? (v22)*

▷ *Do you work harder only when someone's watching?*

▷ *Why should Christians work hard? What's their motivation? (v23–24)*

Paul says: Go for it! Obey your "boss", even if they annoy you. Don't work hard just to keep them happy but give your all as if you're working for God (v23). You are! It's not about the money you earn or the grades you get here on earth. It's about serving Jesus with your whole being, giving everything for Him. He has already promised Christians their reward — eternal life with Him (v24).

Working your socks off is a way of showing your gratitude for everything Jesus has done for you and everything you'll receive in eternity.

GET ON WITH IT

▷ *How will you change the way you work this week?*

PRAY ABOUT IT

Ask God to help you work harder for Him. Ask Him to keep reminding you that it's Him you're serving.

THE BOTTOM LINE

Work hard; you're doing it for God.

→ TAKE IT FURTHER

For extra work, page 123.

80 Talking to God

**How are you finding prayer right now? How
often do you talk to God? What do you say?
Paul has been giving us some great advice on
how to live as Christians. Now he turns to prayer...**

👁 **Read Colossians 4 v 2–4**

ENGAGE YOUR BRAIN

▶ *What does it mean to be
devoted to something?*

▶ *How can you be more devoted
to talking to God?*

Yet again Paul says: Go for it! This is
God, the Creator of the universe. And
YOU get to talk to Him! As often as
you want! So what are you waiting
for??? Devote yourself to talking to
your heavenly Father. You've got so
much to thank Him for, so do it (v2).

▶ *What did Paul ask the Colossians
to pray for? (v3–4)*

Paul was in prison for telling people
about Jesus, and he wanted these
Christians to pray for him. To pray
that he would have the opportunity
to tell more people about the
gospel, and that he'd be able to
do it clearly (v4).

We need to pray hard for Christians
we know who spread the gospel.
Anyone spring to mind?

PRAY ABOUT IT

Take longer today to talk to God.
Make a list of things to thank Him
for. Use verses 3–4 to help you pray
for Christians you know who tell
others about Jesus. Ask God to
give you opportunities to spread
the gospel too.

THE BOTTOM LINE

Be devoted to prayer.
Pray for gospel-spreaders.

➔ **TAKE IT FURTHER**

More prayer hints on page 123.

81 Talking about God

Are you a good talker? What do you enjoy chatting about? How good are you at talking about God? Bet that last one silenced you!

As Paul continues to train the Colossian Christians in living for God, he gives them some top talking tips.

Read Colossians 4 v 5–6

ENGAGE YOUR BRAIN

▶ *How should Christians behave towards outsiders — people who don't know Jesus? (v5)*

▶ *What does it mean to be wise in our behaviour towards outsiders?*

Paul says *be wise* — watch how you act. Are you drawing people in to know more about Jesus or pushing them away with the way you behave? Do you take up opportunities to talk about your faith or do you listen to the whooshing sound as the chances fly by? Paul encourages us to grab opportunities with both hands.

▶ *What might conversation that's full of grace and seasoned with salt sound like? (v6)*

Full of grace means full of Jesus — talking about Him and how He's turned your life around.

Full of salt means interesting. Don't bore people to death when you talk about church. Don't make Christianity sound like a list of rules. Not enough salt makes your food too bland; too much is overpowering. Get the balance right. Try to be lively and interesting in conversation when you're talking about Christian stuff.

SHARE IT

Time to go for it! How will you mention God more in your daily conversations? Are you ready to answer people's questions? If not, what can you do about that?

PRAY ABOUT IT

Ask God to help you grab those opportunities!

→ TAKE IT FURTHER

More talk on page 123.

82 | Wrestle mania

We've reached the end of Paul's letter to the Colossian Christians. He's warned them about people who say you need more than Jesus to be a Christian. And he's given them loads of practical advice on living for Christ.

Now some of Paul's friends say "Hi" to the Colossians...

👁 Read Colossians 4 v 7–18

ENGAGE YOUR BRAIN

▷ How is Tychicus described? (v7–8)
▷ Why did Paul send him to Colosse (v8)?

Like Tychicus, all Christians are *fellow-servants*, working for Jesus. Tychicus' job was to encourage these Christians by telling them what Paul and his friends had been going through to spread the message of Jesus. All Christians need encouragement. Which means we all need to be encouragers too.

▷ How does Paul describe Epaphras? (v12)

It was Epaphras who first told these guys about Jesus (Colossians 1 v 7–8), and he was still praying for them. And not just a quick prayer every now and then. He was ***wrestling***

in prayer for them. Prayer can be a struggle and hard work sometimes. It shouldn't be hit-and-run. We should throw ourselves into it, praying intensely for other Christians, as Epaphras did — that they will stick at it, grow in their faith, and be certain of their eternal future with Jesus.

GET ON WITH IT

▷ Which Christian friends can you encourage this week?

Try to pick at least one to encourage in person, one to phone, and one to email.

PRAY ABOUT IT

Now think of three other Christians you know. Pray Epaphras' prayer for them from verse 12.

→ TAKE IT FURTHER

Never read *Philemon*?
Go to page 123.

Student life

Each month in REAL LIVES, we talk to people whose lives have been transformed by Christ. They tell us their stories: some of them amazing, some of them down-to-earth, but all of them showing us how God has a real impact on our lives.

Katie Cole studied Primary Education in Lincoln, UK. We asked her about life as a Christian at university .

What do you find most stressful — exams or coursework?
And why is that?
Coursework. It's even more prolonged pain than exams!!

What difference has being a Christian made to your student life?
Aiming to live my life out fully for Jesus inspires me to do my best in everything, including work and exams. But my relationship with God also means that I have a different perspective on life and my future, believing that, ultimately, my grades and career are in God's hands and He knows what's best for me.

What challenges and encouragements have you experienced?

I think being a Christian student is a flippin HUGE challenge! Most things that the student culture promotes contrast majorly with the way the Bible says we should live. There are constant temptations and areas to slip up in. But there are also loads of precious opportunities to stand out and share with fellow students the difference that God has made in your life .

A massive encouragement for me has been the way that churches welcome, support and adopt us poor students. This is the church family in action! It's also awesome to get involved in *Christian Union (Christian fellowship)* where a bunch of Christian students can not only support and build each

other up, but also unite in sharing the gospel at university. I've been totally overwhelmed by how open students are to hearing about and even accepting what Jesus has done for them. It's AWESOME!

On exam day, how do you handle your nerves and stress?
I have a good old pray, read a psalm and have a cup of tea.

Have you experienced disappointment with exam results?
Yeah, I fluffed my A-level exams a little bit so didn't get into university first time around.

How did you cope with that?
It's hard on the old ego, but God put verses from Proverbs in my head, which both challenged and blessed me loads. It taught me that God is bigger than exam results.

What's your strangest exam experience?
Er, I once raced through an exam and was the first to finish so that I could go watch my friend's important

presentation… a bit stupid but I still passed!

Have there been any instances when you've really felt God's help or guidance in your studies/exams?
I've often had an amazing and unnatural peace during exams and deadlines which I figure is God calming me down. He calmed storms on the sea so I guess a nervous student is easy!

If you could give just one sentence of advice to people cramming for exams, what would it be?
Do your best (I sound like my mother!), have plenty of caffeine and just give it over to God!

Interview taken from **DON'T PANIC! – The Ultimate Exam Survival Kit**, *available from Christians bookshops and www.thegoodbook.com*

83

JONAH
Stormy waters

You probably know the story of Jonah. He's the one who was swallowed by a whale. It's a big fish actually… but that really isn't the point.

Jonah isn't about the big fish. And although it's called Jonah, he isn't even the main character. Like every book in the Bible, it's all about God. He's the hero, and it's God's character that we really need to pay attention to.

As a prophet, it was Jonah's job to bring God's word, His message, to others. Jonah lived in Israel nearly 800 years before Jesus. His usual target audience was the Israelites — God's chosen people.

Read 2 Kings 14 v 23–27

▷ *What did God use Jonah to do? (v25)*

Through Jonah, Israel had seen God keep His promise to them by restoring the land that had been taken from them. Jonah was probably happy living in Israel, delivering such a positive message from God.

However, God's plan extended way beyond Israel to Nineveh and the rest of the world. The problem was that Israel (and Jonah) didn't want others to benefit from God's love in the same way that they had. And especially not their enemies! In their minds, the Lord was their God, and no one else's.

Thankfully, God didn't exactly agree, and His mission (to show **all** people their need for His rescue) was not about to be scuppered by an unwilling prophet. Can you sense a storm brewing?

PRAY ABOUT IT
Ask God to help you focus on the big point of Jonah over the next week: that God's message is for **everyone**. Ask God to help you share the truth about Jesus with whoever you meet.

THE BOTTOM LINE
It's all about God.
His message is for everyone.

84 | Runaway prophet

How good are you at taking orders?
Are you obedient or rebellious?
What about when the orders are from God?

👁 Read Jonah 1 v 1–3

ENGAGE YOUR BRAIN

▷ *What did God want Jonah to do?*

▷ *Why? (v2)*

▷ *What was Jonah's response? (v3)*

Nineveh was an important city in Assyria, a nation who rejected God and fought the Israelites. The people of Nineveh needed to hear God's message and turn to Him.

But Jonah wouldn't take God's message to Nineveh. Instead, he ran away to Tarshish — which was probably in what is now Spain. It was in the opposite direction from Nineveh.

Later on (Jonah 4 v 2), we're told why Jonah didn't want to go. But we're still left thinking: *"How can Jonah run away from God???"* The temptation is to think Jonah is a bit crazy…

surely we'd never disobey a direct command from God?

THINK IT OVER

Yet, if you're honest, are there some commands in the Bible that you don't pay much attention to? What about honouring your parents, loving your enemies or not wanting other people's stuff?

PRAY ABOUT IT

Ask God to help you obey Him in every part of your life — your thoughts, words and actions — no matter how difficult it might be.

Quickly write a list of areas where you don't obey God. Spend time praying about each of them, saying sorry and asking God's help.

THE BOTTOM LINE

Obey the Lord; don't run away from Him.

➡ TAKE IT FURTHER

But you *can* run away to page 123.

85 Nowhere to run

We've seen how Jonah responded to God — he ran away! But how will God respond to Jonah's rebellion?

👁 Read Jonah 1 v 4–10

ENGAGE YOUR BRAIN

▷ *Did God let Jonah get his own way? What did God do?*

▷ *How did Jonah react? (v5, 9)*

Jonah gives us the ultimate definition of *stubborn*: he runs away from the Lord, sleeps through a storm sent by God, and totally ignores the captain's plea to ask God to spare them! And then he has the nerve to say he worships God (v9)! But Jonah wasn't worshipping God in the way he lived.

GET ON WITH IT

What specific changes can you make so that you're worshipping God in the way you live, and not just saying the right things?

👁 Read verses 11–17

▷ *Did Jonah turn back to God and repent?*

▷ *What did the sailors recognise about God? (v14)*

▷ *How do we see that God's in complete control? (v13, 15, 17)*

We're not told whether Jonah turned back to God at this stage. What is absolutely certain is that **God was in total control**. His original plan for Jonah hadn't changed. Despite Jonah's disobedience, God rescued him with a huge fish. He showed great mercy to Jonah, giving him so many extra chances!

PRAY ABOUT IT

Ask Him to help you to live a life with Him in charge. Glance back at **Get on with it** and pray about those things.

THE BOTTOM LINE

God's in charge, whether we like it or not.

→ TAKE IT FURTHER

For more, dive into page 124.

86 | Nowhere to hide

It's a pretty strange place to find yourself, in a fish's stomach... Now we find out just how and why that happened, and notice a big change in our man Jonah.

👁 **Read Jonah 2 v 1–10**

▷ *What happened to Jonah? (v3, 5)*

▷ *What was his response? (v2, 7)*

▷ *And how did God respond to Jonah's prayers? (v2, 6, 10)*

Finally! Jonah did what he should have done ages ago — he called out to God. Amazingly, the Lord still showed patience with Jonah after his repeated disobedience.

▷ *What word does Jonah use to sum this up in v8?*

Grace (some Bible versions have "love") is when God gives us far more than we deserve. In fact, we deserve the opposite. Jonah realised that he didn't deserve God's grace, yet he also realised that salvation (rescue) only comes from the Lord (v8–9).

Sadly, many people worship other things in their lives (money, relationships, sport, image, good grades etc) instead of accepting God's grace and rescue from sin, and putting Him first.

SHARE IT

Verse 8 is as true for your friends as it was for Jonah, so why don't you plan how you can tell a friend about the grace and rescue that we can have through Jesus?

PRAY ABOUT IT

Thank God that He does answer people who call out to be rescued. Pray for a non-Christian friend, that they would experience God's grace, and the rescue and forgiveness of Jesus.

THE BOTTOM LINE

"Those who cling to worthless idols turn away from God's love for them... Salvation comes from the Lord."

→ **TAKE IT FURTHER**

Go fishing on page 124.

87 | Second chance

After running away and refusing to take God's message to Nineveh, Jonah was given a second chance.

👁 Read Jonah 3 v 1–4

ENGAGE YOUR BRAIN

▶ *The instruction from God is the same, but how is Jonah's response different this time?*

▶ *What was God's message to Nineveh? (v4)*

God hates sin and will punish all those who rebel against Him. The future looked bleak for Nineveh.

👁 Read verses 5–9

▶ *How did the Ninevites respond to Jonah's terrifying news?*

▶ *What hope did they have? (v9)*

The people of Nineveh realised God Himself was speaking to them. They stopped eating, wore uncomfortable sacks, gave up their sinful ways and pleaded with God to forgive them.

They realised they had sinned against God and deserved to be destroyed by Him. They asked God to forgive them and turned away from their evil ways.

Turning *away* from sin and turning *to* God is repentance. It's how you become a Christian.

▶ *Know anyone who needs to do that? Maybe yourself?*

👁 Read verse 10

God will punish and destroy evil. But He's also a God of incredible love. Here, He forgave the Ninevites and didn't destroy them. And God offers forgiveness to anyone who turns away from their evil ways and trusts in Jesus' death in their place.

SHARE IT

▶ *Who can you tell about the message of God's anger against sin and His offer of forgiveness?*

PRAY ABOUT IT

Thank God for His compassion, especially to you. Pray for His compassion on friends/family who don't yet live for Him.

→ TAKE IT FURTHER

For a second chance, go to page 124.

88 | All inclusive

God showed amazing compassion and didn't destroy Nineveh. Imagine the parties in Nineveh! And the relief. Everyone was happy. Well, not quite everyone...

👁 Read Jonah 4 v 1–3

ENGAGE YOUR BRAIN

▶ Why was Jonah angry and why had he run away earlier? (v2)

▶ How do you feel about Jonah's anger?

Jonah saw everything from his own point of view, not God's. He hated the idea of the Ninevites turning to God. They were Israels' enemies — surely they should be destroyed, not forgiven.

👁 Read verse 4

▶ What's the right answer to God's question?

▶ Why?

Jonah seems to have forgotten that he had run away and refused to obey God. He had deserved to be destroyed. But when he cried out to the Lord, God rescued him!

And God showed the same compassion to the people of Nineveh when they cried out to be rescued from destruction. God is compassionate, fair, and consistent. God always gets it right!

Jonah didn't seem to understand that God cares for all people, not just the Israelites. That's one of the big messages from this book (and the whole Bible): God wants **everyone** to turn to Him and find forgiveness.

GET ON WITH IT

If God cares for everyone, how should this affect the way you view other people? What about those people you can't stand? What do you need to change?

PRAY ABOUT IT

Ask God to help you see people the way He does. And to make your priorities the same as His.

→ TAKE IT FURTHER

Feel the love on page 124.

89 | Vine whine

> **Jonah:** God, you're so loving, I knew you'd forgive the Ninevites. It's so annoying!
> **God:** Have you any right to be angry, Jonah?

👁 Read Jonah 4 v 5–9

ENGAGE YOUR BRAIN

▷ What was Jonah hoping would happen to Nineveh? (v5)

▷ Did Jonah deserve the vine? (v6)

▷ So, was his answer to God's question true? (v9)

It's easy to think we deserve things from God. We don't. At all. Yet God does so much for us anyway, because of His great love for us.

Read verses 10–11

How are God's priorities and Jonah's priorities different?

▷ So what's the answer to God's question at the end of v11?

Jonah didn't deserve the vine and he had no right to be angry about it dying. 120,000 people were far more important than a desert plant! Even though they were enemies of the Israelites, God still showed great love for the people of Nineveh.

TALK IT THROUGH

We've seen how God's priorities are very different from Jonah's, and probably ours. Talk with a friend about how your youth group or church can reach those who, like the Ninevites, haven't heard about God's judgment, love and compassion.

PRAY ABOUT IT

Thank God for His plan for people to know Him. Thank Him for sending Jesus to make this possible. Ask God to help you warn people of His judgment and tell them about His amazing love.

→ TAKE IT FURTHER

Stop whining; go to page 125.

90 : Rise and shine

How do you like to start the day? Up at dawn for a two-mile run and a bowl of muesli? Or a long lie-in before crawling into the shower?

👁 Read Psalm 5 v 1–3

David is having trouble with enemies again. So he starts his day by talking to God and asking for His help (v3). And expecting an answer!

▷ *How would starting your day off with God benefit your life?*

David says there are two kinds of people — those hated by God and those accepted by God…

👁 Read verses 4–6 and 9–10

ENGAGE YOUR BRAIN

▷ *From these verses, describe God's enemies in one sentence.*

▷ *How does God treat those who rebel against Him? (v4–6)*

David's enemies are God's enemies. It's not wrong to pray against people who do evil. That doesn't mean praying against people who get

on your nerves, but those who are fighting against God and His people.

👁 Read verses 7–8 and 11–12

Brilliant news! God's people are allowed into His presence (v7); God leads them in the right way to live (v8); they are protected by Him (v11); He shows them great favour (v12). There's every reason to celebrate! Being one of God's people is a fantastic privilege!

PRAY ABOUT IT

▷ *Will you set your alarm a little earlier this week, so you start your day by talking to God?*

Make a list of many of the great privileges of being a Christian, and thank God for them every morning before you launch into your day.

➡ TAKE IT FURTHER

Rise and shine for more on prayer on page 125.

91 | Pain relief

Guess what! King David is having a hard time again. In pain, ill, hounded by his enemies. Let's listen in on his painful groans...

👁 Read Psalm 6 v 1–7

ENGAGE YOUR BRAIN

▷ David was worried that God might be against him. How did this make him feel? (v2–3, 6–7)

▷ Why would the Lord rescue David? (v4)

When you've let God down, how do you feel? David was incredibly upset at the thought that he'd offended God. He wouldn't rest until he knew the Lord's forgiveness and healing.

We can sometimes be arrogant and think we deserve God's help. David knew this wasn't the case. If God rescued him, it was because of His unbeatable love (v4), nothing else.

👁 Read verses 8–10

▷ After talking to God, what was David confident of?
v9:
v10:

PRAY ABOUT IT

David knew he didn't deserve to be rescued by God. And we don't deserve rescue from sin. It's only because of God's great love that He sent Jesus to die for us, so that we can be rescued from the punishment we deserve. Talk to God now and tell Him exactly how that makes you feel.

TALK IT THROUGH

What's getting you down? What sin are you feeling bad about? Grab some Christian friends you trust, and bring these things before God in prayer, confident that He will answer your cries.

➔ TAKE IT FURTHER

For further pain relief, take two tablets, three times a day and go to page 125.

92 | Fair enough

"Life's not fair!" "Why do bad people seem to get away with evil and do well in life?" Well, David says they don't get away with it at all...

👁 Read Psalm 7 v 1–10

ENGAGE YOUR BRAIN

▷ *What did David do when his enemies were after his blood? (v1)*

▷ *What did David want God to do? (v6–7)*

As God's chosen king, David's enemies were God's enemies. They were out to kill David and were rejecting God. David asked God to rescue him (v1) and knew the Lord would keep him safe (v10).

David didn't seek revenge on his bloodthirsty enemies. He left it to God to deal with them.

👁 Read verses 11–17

▷ *Will evil people get away with it?*

▷ *What will happen to them? (v16)*

God is completely fair. It's not for us to get revenge on people who wrong us. In the end, God treats everyone fairly. People who choose to live without God will ultimately end up frustrated (v14), trapped (v15) and causing their own downfall (v16). Justice will be done!

GET ON WITH IT

Who treats you badly? How can you make sure you act in a godly way towards them, not seeking revenge? Will you hand the situation over to God and ask Him to deal with it?

PRAY ABOUT IT

God is completely fair. He is perfect. So we should thank Him and praise His name (v17). Right NOW.

THE BOTTOM LINE

Justice will be done. By our perfect, completely fair God.

→ TAKE IT FURTHER

The final one of this issue, page 125.

TAKE IT FURTHER

If you want a little more at the end of each day's study, this is where you come. The TAKE IT FURTHER sections give you something extra. They look at some of the issues covered by the day's study, pose deeper questions, and point you to the big picture of the whole Bible.

PSALMS:
Psongs from the heart

1 – TWO KINDS OF PEOPLE

Not sure which way you're living? Check out **Galatians 5 v 22–26** for the kind of fruit that should be ripe in our lives. Why not ask a close friend if they think you're growing as a Christian. Maybe you can start meeting regularly to encourage each other, read the Bible and pray together.

2 – WHO'S THE BOSS?

After Jesus had gone back to heaven, Peter and John were persecuted for telling people about Him. **Check out Acts 4 v 23–31.** They quoted Psalm 2 as encouragement that God was in control even through the tough times.

▷ *Know any Christians who are being hassled for their faith?*

▷ *How can you encourage them?*

4 – NIGHT NIGHT

David mentions making right sacrifices to God (v5). People made sacrifices to God to ask for forgiveness from Him.

Turn to 1 John 2 v 1–2. Jesus was the ultimate sacrifice. He died on the cross to take the punishment for our sins. If we trust in His death, we're forgiven for ever! (And that offer is open to EVERYONE.)

JOHN 1–3:
Signs of life

5 – THE WORD OF LIFE

Read Genesis 1 v 1–5

▷ *Who else is described as being present along with the Father and the Son at creation?*

Just as Jesus (*the Word*) is the originator of life in creation, so the Holy Spirit, is the very breath of creation.

6 – GOODBYE DARKNESS, HELLO LIGHT

The Jews in Jesus' day were very proud of their ancestors. Later on, John records an incident where they argue with Jesus about being Abraham's children (John 8 v 31–41).

Read Isaiah 63 v 7–19
- *What exciting and encouraging things did God do for His children in "days of old"?*
- *What clues are there that this relationship was spoiled?*

Paul knew all this. When he wrote to the Galatians, he had to explain to them what it really meant to be God's children. **Read Galatians 3 v 26-29.** What does Paul say here about belonging to God?

7 – IN TENTS STUFF
In the Old Testament, no one was allowed to see God's glory. Moses asked in **Exodus 33 v 18-23**.
- *What was God's reply?*

Eventually, Moses saw God's back and heard Him announce His character (Exodus 34 v 5-7). The result was that Moses had to hide his own face because it reflected God's glory! (Exodus 34 v 29-35)

But now **we** can see God's glory. **John 1 v 14** can be true for us all, because we can get to know Jesus.
- *How are you going to do that?*

8 – CENTRE OF ATTENTION
The people were confused about John but they knew their Old Testament. They were trying to identify John from the old prophecies.

Read Deuteronomy 18 v 14–22
A prophet is not someone who predicts the future, but is someone who delivers God's message. Read through that passage again and write down anything that applies to **Jesus**.

Jesus was God's ultimate messenger — we must listen to Him.

9 – JESUS — THE FACTS
John the Baptist points to Jesus as the one who will take away the sin of the world. In the Old Testament, one of the symbols of the removal of sin was the *scape goat*.

Read Leviticus 16 v 20–22
Think about the cross.
- *How does Jesus carry all our sins to be removed for ever?*

10 – MESSIAH MESSAGE
Peter, the rock, went on to play a big role in the early church (see the first half of Acts). Full of the Holy Spirit, Peter became a great speaker. What was his message? (**Acts 2 v 36–41**)

Think about Peter's humble beginnings and the way God used him. It's both encouraging and a little scary to know that God uses His people in amazing, surprising ways.
- *How might God use you today?*
- *Are you ready?*

11 – CLOSE TO HOME
John 1 v 51 reminds us of when Jacob dreamed of a stairway reaching up to heaven. **Read about it in Genesis 28**

v 10–22. In the dream, the covenant (agreement) God made with Abraham is repeated for Jacob. It showed God's grace in opening the way back to Himself.

Now Jesus repeats the phrase for Nathanael. Jesus is the only way to heaven, the real stairway. The same covenant that God made with Abraham, Isaac and Jacob is ours because of Jesus. That's great news, Jesus told Nathanael. Do you think so too? Nathanael followed Jesus... Jacob made a special vow...

▷ *How will you respond to God's grace?*

12 – A WEEK IN THE LIFE

Who was the Son of Man? **Daniel 7 v 9–14** gives us the clues that we need. Read it. Daniel 7 is a vision about who is really in charge.

▷ *Who does God (the Ancient of Days) give all authority to?*
▷ *What else do we discover about the Son of Man?*

By calling Himself the Son of Man, Jesus is identifying Himself with this character from Daniel. He really is the person to whom all authority, glory and power belong. That's pretty awesome. Spend time thanking God for who Jesus is.

13 – WINE SIGN

A few days ago we saw that in Jesus we can see God's glory (John 1 v 14). By changing water into wine, Jesus revealed His glory (2 v 11). By revealing His glory, the miracle is a signpost pointing out that

Jesus is God. The servants at the wedding see the sign, not the glory. The disciples see both and put their faith in Jesus. Not everyone who sees the sign sees the glory. As John's gospel gradually reveals Jesus' glory, there will be rejection along the way. The ultimate sign of Jesus' glory, His death on the cross, also divides people.

▷ *How do your friends respond to Jesus' death on the cross?*
Pray about that now.

14 – TEMPLE TEMPER

In Exodus, a tent is made called the Tent of Meeting. Later, when the Israelites are settled in Canaan, the tent becomes a temple. The people have the amazing privilege of being able to meet with God in the temple. However, on many occasions they either take it for granted or worship other gods.

Later on, God speaks through the prophet Haggai to warn them about ignoring God's house.
Read Haggai 1 v 1–6
▷ *What have the people been doing instead of rebuilding the temple?*

The problem in Haggai's time, and when Jesus cleared the temple, was a contempt for meeting with God. It came lower down on the priority list than personal comfort or making money. Now that we can meet God through Jesus, ask yourself how high that comes on your list of priorities.
▷ *Are you letting anything come*

between you and your relationship with God?

15 – BIRTH DAY

Check out Ezekiel 36 v 25–27

God promised the Israelites a new birth, a new start. 600 years later, Jesus told Nicodemus he needed to be born again.

🔹 *For Christians, what does it mean to have a new heart, a new life?*

🔹 *How does **your** life show you've been born again?*

🔹 *What do you still need the Holy Spirit's help to change?*

GENESIS:
In the beginning

16 – BEFORE THE BEGINNING

Find the verses in **Genesis 1** that answer these commonly-held views:
a) Everything was created just by chance.
b) The stars (horoscopes) affect your destiny.
c) God is just something inside everyone.

17 – FILLING THE VOID

The big point being made in **Genesis 1 and 2** is that God made the world and us. How He did it is not the main focus of these chapters, and Christians have different views on this.

While we all agree that God is the Creator, some think God made the world in six 24-hour periods, while others believe that he

took years and years to do it.
If you're interested in this debate, why not check out this weblink: http://www.bethinking.org and go to the *Science & Christianity* section.

18 – WHAT A WONDERFUL WORLD

Read Colossians 1 v 15–17

🔹 *How great does this make Jesus?*

Read Revelation 21 v 1–4

🔹 *What will God's new world be like?*

19 – CREATING AN IMAGE

🔹 *If all humans are made in God's image, what should that mean for the way we treat each other?*

🔹 *How about the vulnerable, the terminally ill, the unborn baby?*

20 – UNDER A REST

Now's your chance to read up on the promises of rest for those who trust in Christ.
Matthew 11 v 28–30
Hebrews 4 v 9–11
Revelation 14 v 13

21 – EXTREME CLOSE-UP

If you're a Christian, God has not only given you life, but also new life.

Read John 3 v 1–21

Trusting in Jesus means we are born again. We can have the *"breath of life"* that God's Spirit gives.

🔹 *How does that affect the way you live?*

22 – GARDEN PARTY

Have a look at the perfect paradise God has planned for eternity. **Check out Revelation 21 v 1 – 22 v 5.**

▷ *Can you spot any similarities to Eden? Jot down anything that surprises or amazes you.*

23 – WOULD YOU ADAM AND EVE IT?

Verse 24 is very important — Jesus refers to it, as does Paul. The relationship between husband and wife is so special because it reflects God's relationship with His people.

Check out **Ephesians 5 v 21–33** for one example.

24 – IT'S ALL GONE BELLY UP

The snake is not just a snake. Check out **Revelation 12 v 9–10** for his true identity.

▷ *How does the devil tempt you to rebel against God?*
Talk to God about it.

25 – FREE FALLING

There is a glimmer of hope in this depressing chapter — check out v15. There will be a descendant of the woman who will crush the serpent's head. The rest of the Bible shows the hunt for this *serpent crusher* who will defeat the devil.

Check out Psalm 91 v 11–16 and Matthew 4 v 1–11

26 – DIE ANOTHER DAY

God's mercy doesn't finish here with a couple of fur coats and a postponed death sentence. One day, mankind will return to God's presence in a renewed Eden because of Jesus (*the Lamb*).
Read Revelation 22 v 1–6

27 – OH BROTHER...

The New Testament gives us an explanation of why Cain's sacrifice wasn't acceptable. **Read Hebrews 11 v 4 and 1 John 3 v 12.** God is always concerned with our hearts, our motives.
Check out **Hosea 6 v 6** and **Psalm 51 v 16–17** as well.

28 – THE GOOD, THE BAD, AND THE UGLY

A pattern of sin–judgment–grace is repeated throughout Genesis 1–3. In chapter 3, Adam and Eve rebel against God's word (sin), and are kicked out of Eden (judgment) but are allowed to live (grace).

In chapter 4, Cain murders Abel (sin), and is driven away (judgement), but Eve gives birth to Seth and many generations follow (grace). We'll see the pattern again in Genesis 6–9.

▷ *What does this pattern tell us about God?*

AMOS:
God's the boss

29 – ROAR MATERIAL

God is also described as a roaring lion in **Isaiah 31 v 4–5**.

▶ *What other part of God's character do we see here (v5)?*

▶ *How do God's anger and rescue go hand in hand (Romans 6 v 23)?*

30 – NASTY NEIGHBOURS

▶ *What is God's relationship with the nations of the world?*

Romans 1 v 18–20, Psalm 117 v 1–2, Matthew 28 v 16–20

31 – SPOT THE DIFFERENCE

Israel had broken their covenant agreement with God. They were living their own way, not His.

▶ *In what ways do we sometimes act like the Israelites?*

Read Hebrews 10 v 26–39

▶ *What hits you hard?*

▶ *What encouragement can Christians take (v35–39)?*

32 – SPECIAL TREATMENT

Our God is the judge (v2). He judges the nations by what they can know of Him from the world He's made (**see Romans 1 v 18–20**). And He judges the people He's revealed Himself to by a higher standard.
Check out Hebrews 10 v 26–31.

To be chosen by God means being different from people who don't know Him.

▶ *Is that true of you?*

▶ *In what ways?*

33 – SILLY COWS

▶ *What does Amos call God in v2 and v5?*

▶ *Any idea what that means?*

God is the *Sovereign Lord* who controls everything that happens in the universe.
See Isaiah 45 v 5–7 and Psalm 113.
God's in charge.

34 – WARNING SIGNS

Verse 13 paints a powerful picture of God. See **Job 38 v 1 – 40 v 5** for a more detailed portrait of God.

▶ *What should be our response to almighty God?*

▶ *Are you ever too "familiar" or disrespectful to the Creator of the universe?*

35 – DEAD SERIOUS

Verses 1–3: Had God really given up on Israel??? What about His covenant agreements with them (Genesis 12 v 1–3)?
See Amos 5 v 15: God would judge Israel, but there would be rescue and forgiveness for the remaining few. God's judgment gets rid of the false members of His people, so that the true ones remain.
See 2 Thessalonians 1 v 5–10.

36 – LOSING YOUR RELIGION

Slowly read **2 Corinthians 5 v 17–21**, then throw yourself into prayer.

- Thank Jesus for making His people right with God.
- Say sorry for times when you only appear to be living His way, not actually doing it.
- Pray that your relationship with God would affect your relationships at home/school/work.

37 – EASY LIFE?

Read Mark 10 v 35–45

- *What do James and John think about power and fame?*
- *What is Jesus' view?*
- *What's His ultimate example (v45)?*

38 – PRIEST V PROPHET

Often the stiffest opposition can come from within the church, from "Christians". Amos was opposed by a priest, and Jesus by religious leaders (John 10 v 22–39).

Sadly, we can't just assume that everything we hear in Christian meetings is straight from God. We have to check it with what the Bible says.

- *What attitudes about the Bible have you heard that you feel are wrong?*

Now get working on how to answer them!

39– SILENT PLIGHT

Verse 14 — they worshipped false gods instead of the real God. People who refuse to hear God's word and obey it will find other things to fill the gap.

- *What examples can you think of (eg: horoscopes, tarot cards)?*
- *What can you say to friends who rely on other things rather than God?*

40 – NO ESCAPE

Still worried about the judgment thing?
Check out Matthew 25 v 31–46

That's the test — if our faith is real, we'll show love and care for other Christians. The Israelites relied on God's choice of them in the past and forgot how much God hates sin. Amos said: "*Keep living for God*". The rest of the Bible says: "*Keep trusting Jesus' death in your place*". And not our own past experiences or achievements.

41 – FUTURE FANTASTIC

- *How would you sum up Amos' message about the future?*

Read 2 Samuel 7 v 8–16 and Revelation 11 v 15

- *How will Amos' message come true?*
- *Are you keeping yourself prepared for Jesus' return?*

JOHN 3–5

42 – SIGNS OF LIFE

Light is a strange thing. Put a bright light outside at night and moths and other bugs will come and gather round it. For other animals, light is danger; they'll stay away from the light and stick to the safety of the shadows. As with light, so it is with Jesus — the light of the world.

Read 1 John 1 v 5–7

▷ *What are the two places that people "walk"?*

We are not naturally like the moths. We do not like the light. Instead we prefer to walk in the darkness and ignore God. Sometimes we may claim to love God, but are really walking in darkness. Use **1 John 1 v 6** now to check your own "walk" and pray to God about it.

43 – THE BEST MAN'S SPEECH

The Bible says that eternal life will be like a wedding feast.

Read Revelation 19 v 6–9

▷ *What will that wedding party be like?*
▷ *How do you think you get invited (v9)?*

Turn the page and read **Revelation 21 v 1–4**. Just as when a couple get married they are joined together as one family, one day God will be with His people for ever.

▷ *What does verse 4 say that will be like?*

Ask God to help you prepare for the wedding. Ask Him to help you fix your mind on those wonderful events that are yet to come, as He helps you live for Him in the here and now.

44 – THIRST QUENCHER

Read Ezekiel 36 v 25–27. Here, God is promising His people clean water to purify them and the Spirit to help them live God's way.

▷ *What does v27 say the Spirit does?*

Through Jesus we receive purification and new life when we become Christians. We're washed clean of our sins and given a new Spirit-filled life.

Ask God to help you live for Him with the help of the Holy Spirit.

45 – TRUE WORSHIP

You might have sung the song *"Come, now is the time for worship"*. It's often used to start church services as we encourage each other to praise God together. Perhaps, though, the song should be sung at the end of a service. It's easy to praise God in a large group on Sunday. It's not so easy to praise and worship God when we're by ourselves and under pressure from the world.

The *"time for worship"* is all the time.

Read Romans 12 v 1–2

▷ *What sort of "act of worship" do we offer to God?*
▷ *What do you think it means to "not*

conform … to the pattern of this world"?

Talk to God about the areas of your life where you need His transformation so that you can truly worship Him.

46 – HEARING IS BELIEVING

Jesus' *food* is to obey God (v34). For Jesus, doing the will of the Father was as essential to life as His daily meals.

▶ *Do you consider obedience to God to be so important?*

Read the Lord's Prayer in Matthew 6 v 9–13. We're told to ask for our daily bread directly after asking for God's will to be done *"on earth as it is in heaven"*. One of the ways that God's will is done is through our obedience. So in the same breath we are asking for bread and promising obedience.

Would it seem right to rely on God for daily food and then be disobedient? Thank God now that He provides for your daily needs and ask Him to help you obey Him more.

47 – WORD'S WORTH

God does everything at just the right time. **Read Romans chapters 6–8.** Thank God for His perfect timing in sending Jesus.

49 – GET UP AND GO

The New Testament encourages us to respond to sickness with prayer — see **James 5 v 13–15**. But it can sometimes be confusing when God doesn't make

our friends well again instantly. Firstly, remember that instant healing is not promised. Paul prayed earnestly for his *"thorn in the flesh"* to be removed and it wasn't (**2 Corinthians 12 v 7–10**). We are not promised a life without sickness or sorrow.

It's even more important to pray for spiritual healing. When Paul writes to churches, he almost always tells them he's praying for their spiritual growth and rarely mentions physical healing.

Think about the balance of your prayers — do you spend enough time praying for the spiritual health of your Christian and non–Christian friends? Pray now about some of your friends.

50 – FAMILY BUSINESS

Hebrews 4 v 8-11 tells us that the Sabbath rest also points us forward to the time of ultimate rest, eternal life.

We no longer keep the seventh day, but the first day of the week, Sunday. You may or may not be strict about what you do. But pray that God will help you live life now, always looking forward to the hope of eternal life.

51 – WAKING THE DEAD

The Bible makes it clear that Jesus will be the Judge at the end of time. **Read Acts 17 v 30–31** God will judge with justice through the man He has appointed — Jesus.

▷ *How has God given proof that this will happen (v31)?*

52 – WITNESS FOR THE DEFENCE
Read John 20 v 30-31 and John 3 v 36
John wants us to see that you can't sit on the fence. There is no middle ground when it comes to believing in Jesus. If you don't believe in Jesus, you are rejecting Him. Think about some of the people that we have read about — Simon and Andrew, Nathanael, Nicodemus and the Samaritan woman.

▷ *How was each of them challenged about not sitting on the fence?*
▷ *What difference did Jesus make to each of their lives?*
▷ *Have you made up your mind about Jesus?*

Ask God for help to believe and trust in Jesus, His Son. Ask God to help you stop rejecting Jesus in any part of your life.

GENESIS 5–11

53 – IN THE BEGINNING
Death was not part of God's original design. It's horrible. Jesus came to destroy death; those who trust in Him will enjoy eternal life with God for ever — **read 1 Corinthians 15 v 20–26**.

54 – GRIEVING GOD
Things today aren't much different from Noah's day. Watch the news, read the papers and look again at verse 5. There's a warning for us today too, especially for those who don't follow Jesus — **see Matthew 24 v 36–44**.

▷ *What's the big warning?*

55 – ARK AND RIDE
Look at v18 again. This is the first time God talks about establishing *"a covenant"* with people. A covenant was a relationship, a commitment to someone. He's making a promise to rescue them. Can you think of any other covenants in the Bible?
Check out:
Genesis 12 v 1–3
Deuteronomy 4 v 12–14
2 Samuel 7 v 8–16
Jeremiah 31 v 31-34
Luke 22 v 14–20

56 – FLOOD WARNING
Look again at verse 1.
▷ *Do you think Noah was perfect?*
▷ *Did God save him because he was righteous?*

Skip forwards to **Genesis 15 v 6** and then **Hebrews 11 v 7** for a definition of what righteous might mean here and then look at verse 5 again.

58 – A FRESH START
God promised not to wipe out all life by a flood again, but only as long as the earth endures (v22)...

Check out 2 Peter 3 v 1–14
When Jesus returns, the old world will be

destroyed and those who've rejected God will be punished. God's people will live with Him on the the new earth.

▶ *What effect should this have on us now (v14)?*

59 – LIFEBLOOD

Check out these verses on hate — 1 John 2 v 9-11, 1 John 3 v 15
▶ *Anything you need to do?*

60 – PROMISES PROMISES

One of the purposes of communion / the Lord's Supper is to act as a sign — a bit like the rainbow. Read **1 Corinthians 11 v 23–26** and work out what promise it reminds us of.

61 – DRUNK AND DISORDERLY

▶ *Is drinking alcohol wrong?*
▶ *Or just getting drunk?*

Check out the following passages and see for yourself what the Bible has to say: **John 2 v 1–11, Ephesians 5 v 18, 1 Corinthians 6 v 12 and 8 v 13.**
▶ *What are the dangers of drinking alcohol for a Christian?*

63 – BABEL BABBLE

Babel ended up as Babylon — an enemy country full of foreign gods, where God's people were taken as prisoners when they disobeyed Him. Babylon is often used as code in the Bible for the world, which rejects God, the world that is intent on glorifying itself, full of people wanting to

make a name for themselves.
Check out Revelation 18 v 1–24.

COLOSSIANS

65 – HOW TO GROW A CHRISTIAN

The Colossian Christians were great at showing love to others.
▶ *Who helped them to be so loving (v8)?*

In his letter to Christians in Galatia, Paul talks about fruit produced in Christians by the Holy Spirit. **Check out Galatians 5 v 22–26.** The Holy Spirit is with all Christians, helping them to live God's way.

▶ *What else does the Spirit help Christians to show, as well as love? (Galatians 5 v 22–23; 2 Timothy 1 v 6–7)*

66 – THE KNOWLEDGE

▶ *Are you clear about what the gospel is?*
▶ *Try to summarise v12–14 in your own words.*

Now dip into **1 Corinthians 15 v 1–6** to read another summary of the gospel by Paul. If we want to share it, we need to know it!

67 – NUMERO UNO

We can't see God, so how can we know what He's like (v15)? Compare v15 with what you read a few weeks ago in John (John 1 v 18).

And remember in Genesis, how humans are created in God's image (Genesis 1 v 27)? Look at **Colossians 1 v 15** again. Jesus was the perfect man. He is everything that someone made in the image of God should be.

▶ *How can you be more like Jesus?*

68 – BEFORE AND AFTER

Read 2 Corinthians 5 v 17–21

▶ *How is the before and after described here?*

Reconciliation is bringing people back together after a breakdown in their relationship.

▶ *Which relationship was broken and what did God do about it?*

▶ *So what is the Christian's responsibility (v20)?*

69 – SOLVING THE MYSTERY

Read verses 28–29 again. Paul was working hard to look after younger Christians, like these ones in Colosse.

Think of younger Christians you know. Work out practical ways you can aid them in becoming more mature Christians.

▶ *What will help them grow in their faith?*

▶ *How can you help in that?*

70 – WHAT'S THE SECRET?

A friend asks you what the Christian life is all about — what does being a Christian mean, day by day?

▶ *Would you be able to answer them?*

▶ *Why / why not?*

▶ *As your answer to them, re-write Colossians 2 v 6–7 in your own words. Try to leave out any Christian-y jargon!*

71 – CUT IT OUT!

Read Galatians 5 v 19–21 and 24–26

In Colossians and Galatians, Paul tells Christians that, with the Holy Spirit's help, they must put off their old sinful nature.

▶ *From v19–21, what specifically do you need to cut out?*

72 – NAILING THE TRUTH

Paul says Christians used to be dead in their sins but now they're alive in Christ.

Read Ephesians 2 v 1–5

▶ *What were we like when we were "dead" (v1–3)?*

▶ *How is God described, who raised us to life with Jesus (v4–5)?*

73 – CHASING SHADOWS

The false teachers pretended to be more humble than they were (v18).

▶ *Ever fall into that trap yourself?*

They worshipped angels (v18).

▶ *Is there anything that pushes Jesus from the number one spot in your life?*

They had loads of made–up rules about what you CAN'T do (v21). Do you ever get so obsessed with what you shouldn't do that you don't actually do the positive things we're urged to as Christians? (**Matthew 5 v 43 – 6 v 15** for some pointers.)

74 – BACK TO THE FUTURE

Read Philippians 3 v 12–21

▶ *What is the incredible prize that Christians press on towards (v14)?*

▶ *What's true of people who reject Christ, whose minds are on earthly things (v18–19)?*

▶ *How are Christians different (v20–21)?*

75 – GET IT SORTED

Go back to **Colossians 2 v 6–7** and see the number of times after that in chapters 2 and 3 that Paul says *"Since..."* or *"Therefore..."* It's all linked together! In 2 v 6–7 Paul describes the Christian life and then follows it up with the specifics of what it means to live as a Christian.

Chapters 3 and 4 give instructions for Christian living as individuals (3 v 5–11), as Christians together (3 v 12–17), at home (3 v 18–21), at work (3 v 22 – 4 v 1) and with outsiders (4 v 2–6). Why not read the whole of Colossians and see how it all links together? Check out the big picture.

76 – HOLY WARDROBE

Paul says that it's love that ties together all the good qualities of a Christian. Check out **1 Corinthians 13 v 1–13**, and make a note of...

• the stuff that's familiar to you
• anything that's new or mind-blowing
• how you can better show this kind of love to people around you.

77 – BODY LANGUAGE

Paul gives top tips on Christian living in all of his letters. **Read Ephesians 5 v 15–21.**

▶ *What's different from Colossians, and what's similar?*

▶ *How can we show our thankfulness to God?*

▶ *In what ways can we "submit" to and show respect for other believers (v21)?*

78 – FAMILY FORTUNES

Check out Galatians 3 v 28

Men and women are equal in Christ!

Now read **Ephesians 5 v 22–33** for fuller teaching on the marriage thing.

▶ *What comparison is made in v23?*

A Christian wife should honour her husband as head of the family, just as all Christians submit to Jesus as head of the Christian family.

That doesn't mean men and women aren't equal as Christians! In fact, husbands are warned not to take advantage or treat their wives badly. They must love their wives in the same selfless way that Jesus loves us, prepared to give their lives for their wives! And you think a wife's job of submitting to her husband is hard!

79 – WORKING CLASS

Paul says we should work hard for Jesus because we know we'll receive an inheritance from Him (v23–24).

▷ *What is the inheritance that Christians will receive? (Colossians 1 v 12–14, Matthew 19 v 28–30)*

80 – TALKING TO GOD

Paul says be thankful to God as you talk to Him. Thankful for what?

▷ *Make a list from* **Psalm 65** *and* **Psalm 116***, then add a few of your own.*

81 – TALKING ABOUT GOD

Look up Matthew 5 v 13–16

▷ *How does Jesus describe Christians (v13, 14)?*
▷ *What shouldn't Christians do (v13, 15)?*
▷ *How could your conversation be more salty?*
▷ *How can you shine more as a Christian in what you do?*

82 – WRESTLE MANIA

Many of the men Paul mentions at the end of his letter to the Colossians feature in his letter to Philemon. Especially Onesimus (v9). Find the book of **Philemon** in your Bible and read it — it's really short!

▷ *How does Paul urge Philemon to treat Onesimus (v8–17)?*
▷ *Who do you need to forgive and accept as a fellow servant of Christ?*
▷ *How can you treat them better and encourage them?*

When you have time, read through the whole of Colossians in one sitting. Jot down the things that really leap out at you. Write down what you need to be careful of and what positive steps you can take to live more for Jesus.

JONAH

84 – RUNAWAY PROPHET

The beginning of Jonah makes it clear that God won't just turn a blind eye to sin. The book of **Romans** explains that sin is such a big problem because its end result is death (6 v 23). It also tells us that everybody is in the same situation (3 v 23). Everyone needs to turn back to God.

In **Matthew 28 v 19–20**, Jesus gives the command to "go and make disciples of all nations".

▷ *How good are you at keeping this command?*
▷ *How could you make a start with the people around you?*

85 –NOWHERE TO RUN

Read **Jonah 1 v 4–5, 14–16** and compare it with **Mark 4 v 35–41**.

For both the sailors and the disciples, it was not the weather but the power of God that was most terrifying. All of these people saw the One who has complete power over the universe — no wonder they were scared!

▶ *Are there times when you don't take God seriously enough?*

We should have the same respect and awe for Him that the sailors and the disciples expressed when they saw the storms being calmed. And yet, because of Jesus, we can get to know this awesome God personally!

86 – NOWHERE TO HIDE

Read Matthew 12 v 38–41. Jonah's ordeal showed God's rescue and grace to him personally. But Jesus' death and resurrection showed God's grace and rescue to the **whole world**.

The people of Nineveh were going to be forgiven and given hope because Jonah preached to them. This could only happen because he'd been in the big fish for three days. Jesus spending three days in the earth (between His death and resurrection) ultimately gives us the chance of forgiveness, and hope for the future.

Check out **1 Peter 1 v 3–4**, then thank God for what Jesus' death and resurrection means for you.

87 – SECOND CHANCE

Is verse 4 a tip for evangelism? Hit people with the truth about judgment? What about God's love?

When we're telling people about the gospel, we can't talk about God's judgment without mentioning His love. And we can't speak of God's love and miss out His judgment of sin. They go hand in hand.

Work out how you can explain the good news of Jesus, talking about both God's judgment and His love. Practise it out loud! Then take the plunge and pray for natural opportunities to talk about Jesus this week. Look out for them!

88 – ALL INCLUSIVE

It's easy to know about God and His love for others and yet not show that same love ourselves. Jonah was like that (v2).

▶ *In v1–4, what are the differences between Jonah's character and God's?*
▶ *Do you recognise any of Jonah's reactions in yourself?*
▶ *Which ones?*

Ask God to help you show His qualities more and more in your life.

89 – VINE WHINE

As Jonah sat and sulked, the most important thing in his life was his sunshade! When it was taken away, he was totally depressed. His sunshade was far more important to him than 120,000 people dying.

▶ *If you're honest, what are the most important things in your life?*
▶ *What made you happiest this week?*

If it's possessions or achievements rather than people coming to know God, then how do you need to adjust your priorities?

PSALMS 5–7

90 – RISE AND SHINE

David expected God to answer his prayer, and he was prepared to wait for God to answer. **Look up Micah 7 v 7; Psalm 130; Psalm 3 v 4.**

▶ *Do you expect answers to your prayers?*
▶ *Do you notice when God does answer?*

How about keeping a diary of your prayer requests so you can look back and see how God has answered you?

91 – PAIN RELIEF

As always, David is incredibly honest about the way he really feels. What about you?

▶ *What do you hide from other people?*
▶ *What do you try to hide from God?*
▶ *How can you be more honest in the way you talk to God and to other Christians?*

92 – FAIR ENOUGH

For more on God's righteous anger, **read Romans 1 v 18–32**.

engage wants to hear from YOU!

▶ Share experiences of God at work in your life
▶ Any questions you have about the Bible or the Christian life?
▶ How can we make *engage* better?

Email us — **engage@thegoodbook.co.uk**

Or send us a letter/postcard/cartoon/cheesecake to:
Engage, The Good Book Company, Blenheim House,
1 Blenheim Road, Epsom, Surrey, KT19 9AP, UK

In the next engage...

John Meet the real Jesus
Habakkuk God and the garbage
God's great promises in Genesis
Haggai Home truths
Plus: Money issues, 1 Timothy, Psalms
and loads more articles

Order engage now!

Make sure you order the next issue of **engage**. Or even better, grab a one-year subscription to make sure **engage** lands in your hands as soon as it's out.

Call us to order in the UK on 0333 123 0880

or visit your friendly neighbourhood website:
UK: www.thegoodbook.co.uk
N America: www.thegoodbook.com
Australia: www.thegoodbook.com.au
New Zealand: www.thegoodbook.co.nz

DON'T PANIC!

The Ultimate Exam Survival Kit

Exams are a time of real stress for many young Christians – their future resting on their results. It's a time when they most need the guidance and reassurance that God's word can give to them. That's why we've developed **Don't Panic** - a new exam survival guide.

It includes 20 daily Bible readings for stressed-out students, revision timetables, and practical short articles on doing revision, exam technique and dealing with stress. Get hold of a copy of **Don't Panic** for yourself, or for school or college students you know who will be facing exams this summer.